WALKING OF DARKNESS

WALKING IN VALLEYS OF DARKNESS
A BENEDICTINE JOURNEY THROUGH TROUBLED TIMES

Albert Holtz, O.S.B.
Illustrations by the Author

Morehouse Publishing
NEW YORK · HARRISBURG · DENVER

Morehouse Publishing, 4775 Linglestown Road, Harrisburg, PA 17112

Morehouse Publishing, 445 Fifth Avenue, New York, NY 10016

Morehouse Publishing is an imprint of Church Publishing Incorporated.
www.churchpublishing.org

Cover design by Laurie Klein Westhafer
Typeset by Carol Sawyer

Library of Congress Cataloging-in-Publication Data

Holtz, Albert.
  Walking in valleys of darkness : a benedictine journey through troubled times / Albert
Holtz ; illustrations by the author.
     p. cm.
  Includes bibliographical references.
  ISBN 978-0-8192-2739-3 (pbk.)—ISBN 978-0-8192-2741-6 (ebook) 1. Benedictines—
Spiritual life. 2. Spirituality—Catholic Church. 3. Consolation. I. Title.
  BX3003.H58 2011
  248.8'46—dc22

                                      2010044758

Printed in the United States of America

To Bob Holtz

Contents

INTRODUCTION

One of the most basic of all human traits is the desire to make sense of things. We all want to know that our life has a meaning—that it has a plot. Our Judeo-Christian tradition reflects this need when it interprets all of human experience in terms of one single overarching story: God's deep and eternal love for creation, and especially for humankind. Thus the history of the world, the history of the Israelite people, the history of the church, and our own individual lives are all part of the larger story of God's loving plan for us. Our faith assures us that even our worst and most painful experiences are mysteries that actually make sense in terms of God's vast, infinitely loving, plan for us—in particular the central mystery of Christ's suffering, death, and resurrection.

We Benedictines[1] are particularly aware of living within the framework of this sacred story because our lives are immersed in Scripture. Our common public prayer is made up almost entirely of psalms; our private prayer and meditative reading are grounded in Scripture. Saint Benedict's Rule offers a quotation from the Bible as the basis for every one of its practices. Having lived in this Scripture-saturated setting for almost fifty years now, I automatically tend to see things against the backdrop of that great overarching story that is revealed in the Bible.

Some months after the beginning of the economic downturn in 2008, I had to prepare a day of reflection on the topic "A Spirituality for

---

1. Saint Benedict of Nursia (480–540) wrote a "Rule for Monasteries" which still shapes the hearts, minds, and basic spiritual outlook of Benedictine men and women today.

Troubled Times." I found myself naturally interpreting our "troubled times" in terms of the Bible and its story of God's unending love—a story that is always working itself out in our lives, sometimes in ways that we cannot comprehend. I also decided that the idea of "troubled times" could hardly be limited to people's financial hardships, but needed to be expanded to include all the difficulties and struggles we experience in our lives, from the most trivial to the most tragic, from my locking the keys in the car to the doctor telling me I have cancer. "Troubled times" came to refer to any occasion when one is no longer in control.

As you would expect, writing those conferences for that day of reflection gave me an opportunity to reflect on my own periods of struggle and suffering. I'd always thought of my life as being quite pleasant and rather uneventful, and I'd certainly never considered myself someone who had experienced "troubled times." But when I began deliberately looking for difficult periods in my life, I was surprised at how quickly I came up with several of them. The most painful was my brother's death from cancer, which plunged me into a period of grief such as I could never have imagined. Another major catastrophe had come many years before Bob died, when our monastery's school closed in 1972, leaving me numb with shock and sorrow and fearful of my future as a monk and a teacher.

When I looked back on these and other experiences, I noticed a certain pattern: Very often when I had managed to remain grounded in the Lord or to get some perspective or even consolation in a situation, it was thanks to an insight I had gained from meditating on some particular New Testament word in Greek—the original language of the Christian writings.

This is not as strange as it seems. Most of us have certain foreign words that we like to use because they convey better than any English word exactly the meaning or emotion that we want to express. For example, if we were brought up near an Italian neighborhood, the statement "You're giving me *agida!*" says so much more than "You're making me upset." If we're from the New York area, the Yiddish word in the statement "That took a lot of *chutzpah*" probably brings with it all sorts of overtones and feelings that are missing from "He had a lot of nerve." And for most Americans the expression "He was into this *macho* thing" evokes a whole set of unspoken Latino cultural and emotional assumptions that can't really be translated. Sometimes a particularly powerful word such as *karma* or *angst* becomes so meaningful to someone that it shapes the way he or she sees the world and makes decisions. This is exactly the case with me and my Greek words: In my years of studying the Scriptures as a monk and a priest I've come across certain words that have become part of me and have had a pervasive influence on my mind and heart. Maybe I should explain how this happened.

As someone who loves languages (I've taught French, Latin, and Spanish) and who studied Greek in college, I have often turned to my Greek New Testament[2] for insight while meditating on a passage or preparing a homily. Over a period of almost fifty years I have been filling the wide margins of my big Greek New Testament with a marvelous jumble of notes gleaned from commentaries and dictionaries: I've noted dozens of clever puns, words with multiple meanings, and thought-provoking Greek roots. And since I usually try to make my reading of Scripture personal, I have sometimes scrawled next to some particularly powerful word a pointed note to myself such as "Why am I so afraid to try this in my own life?" This is how dozens of Greek New Testament words that I have read and studied over and over have become like old familiar friends, offering me wise insights and timely suggestions that have helped me through some very troubled times.

In the course of the twenty-four reflections that follow I introduce you to many of these "friends" of mine and share with you some of

---

2. The entire New Testament was written originally in Greek. When a New Testament author quotes the Old Testament, in most cases the citation is from the Greek translation of the OT from the original Hebrew done in the 3rd century B.C., known as the Septuagint.

what they've taught me. You'll notice that many of the insights and ideas that I've gleaned from these Greek words simply cannot come through in translation and are destined to lie hidden like buried treasures. The book thus has the added benefit of making these insights available to everyone.

The book is divided into six chapters, the first five of which, arranged in chronological order, correspond to five painful periods in my life. Chapter one tells of the closing of Saint Benedict's Prep in 1972 when I was not yet thirty, an event which left me numb with shock and sorrow. Chapter two deals with an experience several years after that, when I tore a ligament in my knee and underwent serious, painful surgery that left me hobbling around on crutches for eleven long weeks. Then, in chapter three, my brother's death from cancer plunged me into a period of grief such as I could never have imagined, and more recently, as recounted in chapter four, I underwent cancer surgery myself. Chapter five considers the present moment in Newark Abbey's history, as I and my brothers deal with diminishing numbers and wonder what the future will bring. The sixth and final chapter does not address any specific struggle of mine but rather suggests how the Paschal mystery of Christ's redemptive suffering, death, and resurrection offers a life-giving and optimistic perspective that can help us throughout our lives, and especially during troubled times.

It is my fond hope that as you walk with me through some of the dark valleys of my life, you may find a few insights or some encouragement as you deal with your own troubled times. May you come to see more clearly every day that all the events of your life are part of the mysterious story of God's constant, caring, and unconditional love for you, for each one of us, and indeed for all of creation.

CHAPTER ONE

My World Falls Apart
The Closing of Saint Benedict's Prep

The first Benedictine monks I ever met were my teachers at St. Benedict's Prep in Newark. By the end of my freshman year I had already decided that I wanted to become a monk like Father Eugene and Father Benedict and live in that monastery and teach in those classrooms. I did indeed become a Benedictine at nineteen, and after being ordained a priest I did begin teaching at St. Benedict's in 1969. Unfortunately, not long after my arrival, rumors started circulating that our school was in such serious financial difficulties that it might not survive. It was a typical scenario for Catholic institutions in inner-city areas during the early 1970s: a combination of the lack of new monks to replace the ones who were dying or leaving, declining enrollment due to a general disaffection with Catholic education, and "white flight" from the city into the suburbs where new archdiocesan regional high schools were being built. Eventually these factors and others culminated in St. Benedict's closing in the spring of 1972, less than three years after I had started teaching there. I was only twenty-nine and my life had been turned upside down. This was the most devastating event I had ever experienced and it left me dazed and disheartened.

The four reflections that follow, written so many years later, include insights that came to me as I was going through the experience and others that are the fruit of long reflection. But all of them attest to the fact that moments of trial can also be occasions of grace and growth.

1. A Frightening Newness

I LAY THERE IN MY DARK ROOM in the monastery after midnight trying in vain to fall asleep. I just stared at the ceiling as the glow from the streetlights seeped in around the edges of the shades to paint eerie shadows on the ceiling. I'd been lying like this for a couple of hours, too troubled and anxious to sleep. That evening at a meeting of the monastic community, my whole world had suddenly been changed forever: It had been decided that our school would close in June, four months from now.

For almost three years I had been living out my plan, my dream of teaching here at Saint Benedict's Prep, and had assumed that I would continue to do so for the rest of my life. And now that dream was ended, and the future had become a complete blank. From this night onward my future would not be what I'd hoped and planned. I had no idea what was going to happen in my life, except for one thing: It was going to be something completely new.

I had always loved new things, such as putting on a new shirt or starting a new school term with a classroom full of new faces. And the Lord, too, seems to have a fondness for new and unfamiliar situations, starting with the act of creation itself, and then the call of Abraham, calling the Israelites down into Egypt and then out into the wilderness and finally into the promised land. Through the entire New Testament as well the Lord is always up to something new. Saint Paul's repeated call to become a "new being" used to sound like a great idea. The lines "see, everything has become new" (2 Corinthians 5:17) and "[you have] clothed yourselves with the new self" (Colossians 3:10) used to delight me. Until that night. Suddenly I was face to face with an unsettling and even terrifying side of what it means to be "new." I just kept staring at the shadows on the ceiling and trying to make sense of the confused patterns.

Although I didn't know it that night as I lay there haunted by fears and anxieties, I was actually in good company: I was experiencing what our fathers and mothers in the faith had experienced many times in the days of the early church. They had noticed that while newness could sometimes be a source of pleasure, at other times it could be the cause of real suffering. In fact they left us in the New Testament some good insights on newness, including two very different words for new.

One Greek word for new, *neos*,[1] means new in the sense of "recent, young." It's a pleasant enough word used for such things as the "new wine" that gets poured into old wineskins (Luke 5:37). This kind of new describes a new version of something else, as when Jesus is called "the mediator of a new [*neos*] covenant" (Hebrews 12:24). Everything would be great if "new" were limited to this kind of newness. But unfortunately the New Testament idea is complicated by a second word for new, which describes a very different kind of newness.

The other word is *kainos*,[2] new in the sense of something entirely unheard of and unknown, previously un-thought-of, and entirely different from anything that went before. It describes, for instance, the "new self" we need to put on: "put away the old self of your former way of life . . . and put on the new [*kainos*] self, created in God's way in righteousness and holiness of truth" (Ephesians 4:24). This new self is not some cosmetic "makeover" in which we remain essentially unchanged inside (that would be simply *neos*), rather we are being called to be entirely new persons, not *neos* but *kainos*.

Unfortunately it is precisely this unsettling, radical kind of newness that

---

1. *Neos* (neh´-os) is used in such English words as neonatal and neoclassical.
2. *Kainos* (kahee-nos´).

shows up in the most crucial passages of the New Testament, and it was exactly this kind of newness that was keeping me awake that night.

Kainos describes the "new creation" that every Christian already is; "So whoever is in Christ is a new [*kainos*] creation: the old things have passed away; behold new [*kainos*] things have come" (2 Corinthians 5:17). Once again it is clear that God is not interested in freshening us up a bit by simply renovating our old, familiar ways.

Since we cannot be entirely new (*kainos*) while at the same time holding onto our former ways of behaving, one of the key requirements for following Christ and entering the kingdom is openness to being thoroughly transformed.

As I found out that terrible night, the message that "All the old, familiar things have passed away" is frightening and painful; but, as I have continued to discover over and over, being *neos*, "new and improved," is simply not good enough; it is not what we are called to be as Christians. We can draw some comfort however from a vivid vision in the Book of Revelation, written for Christians who were enduring terrible persecution: "the holy city, a new [*kainos*] Jerusalem, coming down out of heaven from God" (Revelation 21:2). The message is clear that even in the midst of appalling suffering—perhaps especially in the midst of such suffering—the transformation of our own world is already under way, just as it was on Calvary. But while we're in the midst of a shattering ordeal, it's nearly impossible to appreciate this newness at work.

I lay there sleepless with worry, still having no idea what God was about to do—except that it would be something new, and not the pleasant kind of new either; it would be something entirely different from anything that had been before—*kainos*.

Small wonder that I never did fall asleep that night.

For Reflection

1. Has God ever called you to a new situation that was not just *neos* (an updated version of some previous situation) but rather *kainos*

(previously un-thought-of)? If so, what did it feel like? How did you respond? Did it change your relationship with God?

2. Reflect for a few minutes on these words of St. Paul: "So whoever is in Christ is a new [*kainos*] creation: the old things have passed away; behold new [*kainos*] things have come" (2 Cor 5:17). Has the Lord been asking you recently to let go of something "old" and familiar in order to make you into a new creation? If so, have you been resisting the change? Welcoming it? Accepting it grudgingly?

Sacred Scripture

Kainos is used also in Mark 1:27, 14:25; John 13:34; Acts 17:19; Gal 6:15; Eph 2:15; Heb 8:8; and Rev 21:1.

Rule of Benedict

Elsewhere Scripture says: O God, you have tested us, you have tried us as silver is tried by fire (Chapter 7, "Humility," v. 40).

2. Finding Courage

I COULD HEAR THE HEAVY OAK CHAIRS SCRAPING on the floor as the rest of the monks stood up and began leaving the long oval table. I had stayed seated, eyes closed, resting my forehead on the table top, slowly shaking my head and moaning inwardly. I'd never been a risk-taker. In fact I'd always prided myself on my measured, cautious approach to life. But that night, Oct. 12, 1972, my cautious side had taken a back seat: We had just voted unanimously to open a new school in our old buildings the following year.

Over the previous five months, since the closing of St. Benedict's Prep, a lot had happened to our community and to me. The mere feat of surviving as a community had given us courage, and we had grown into a unified group determined to stay and live as monks in the city. So under the circumstances it was not completely unreasonable for us to try to put our school facilities and our talents to use once again and attempt to run a school. But I had my head on the table just the same.

Once the decision had been made, the reality of the daunting challenge began to sink in. Next would come, at least for me, the onslaughts of my own timidity and fear. Over the following months and years, as I wrestled with my own fears, I would I ask myself "How can you be afraid if you really believe that God is with you?" Fortunately our mothers and fathers in the faith have left us some helpful insights into how we can confront failure, frustration, and in their case, persecution.

You need to know that the New Testament has two different words for fear. First, there is the common Greek word for fear, *phobos*,[3] giving us our English word "phobia," which can sometimes refer to a fear that is wholesome and productive, such as the fear of the Lord or of someone in authority. But the kind of fear that can paralyze us and keep us from

---

3. *Phobos* (fob´-os), fear, terror.

moving on to the future is better expressed by a second Greek noun, *deilia*,[4] which conveys more the sense of "timidity" or "cowardice." This was what I was feeling that night as I sat there with my forehead on the table in the meeting room.

Jesus used the adjective form of this word when storm waves were threatening to swamp the boat in which the apostles were crossing the lake: "Why are you afraid [*deilos*], O you of little faith" (Matthew 8:26)? The connection is clear, that anyone who is timid and fearful in the face of a threat must be lacking in faith.[5]

To know that our lack of faith is what is behind our worrying is not in itself very helpful or consoling, but fortunately the New Testament offers some practical suggestions for dealing successfully with our cowardice and timidity.

One passage in the Second Letter to Timothy has been particularly helpful to me over the years: "For this reason I remind you to stir into flame the gift of God that you have through the imposition of my hands. For God did not give us a spirit of cowardice [*deilia*], but rather of power and love and self-control" (2 Timothy 1:6–7). Here Paul is contrasting the spirit of cowardice with three qualities of the "spirit" that can help us respond more courageously to the problems and challenges of life. Each of them—power, love, and self-control—can be a help in dealing with our own anxiety.

The first attitude that can help us overcome the spirit of fear, according to Paul, is the "spirit of power." Here the crucial question is, "In this situation, whose power will we automatically rely on, our own or God's?" That night I was naturally thinking only in terms of the limited resources of our little group: our talents, our buildings, and so forth. But if we were going to count only on our own limited, feeble forces, then of course we would run into plenty of situations that

---

4. *Deilia* (dī-lee′-ah), the adjective form is *deilos* (dī-los′), "fearful, timid."

5. At the Last Supper after telling his disciples that he will soon be leaving them, Jesus says: "Do not let your hearts be troubled or afraid [*deilos*]" (John 14:27). In Revelation 21:8 "cowards" [*deilos*] head the list of those destined for punishment.

would threaten to overwhelm us. But in the very next verse Paul offers an alternative to this approach: "relying on the power of God, who saved us" (2 Timothy 1:8). If the power we rely on is not our own but God's, then everything changes, for "I can do all things in Christ, who strengthens me" (Philippians 4:13). We certainly worked hard during the next few months, most of us at jobs outside the monastery, while devoting a lot of energy to community projects and problem solving. But we were all conscious from the start that if our venture was going to succeed it would be because God had made it happen. No matter how much time and effort we spent, ultimately it would all depend on the Lord. From time to time under the pressure of trying to get things done I would forget this truth, but my brothers, through their homilies and conversations always helped me regain my perspective.

The second characteristic that can help us to conquer cowardice is "the spirit of love." John tells us "there is no fear in love" (1 John 4:18). A mother's love makes her capable of heroic actions to save her child from danger even at the risk of her own life. Contrast this with the spirit of self-centeredness, which practically guarantees that everyone and everything will be seen as posing some sort of threat to us. If our small group had felt a need to be in control of everything, then we would have had to live in constant fear that events might get beyond our power, or that our plans would be foiled. But our shared sufferings and frequent meetings and informal conversations had created a bond of caring for one another, making the "spirit of love" a reality in our lives. Because of this intense sense of community, any fears about what might happen to our plans and projects were much easier to handle. I know this was certainly true for me.

The passage from 2 Timothy offers a third quality for countering fear: "self-control." The Greek word, which is sometimes also translated "discipline," means literally "sound-minded."[6] If we let ourselves be controlled by our emotions so that we're always flying off in one

---

6. *Sōphronismos* (sof-ro-nis´-mos), from the roots *sōs*, "safe, sound" and *phrēn*, "mind."

direction or the other, then we will be insecure, unsure of our ground, and thus afraid of what may be lurking around the next bend in the road. I remember how the senior monks were a good example to us younger, more brash, and impetuous members in those first days of planning a school. Eighty-five-year-old Father Celestine, with his heart and mind "firmly grounded in the Lord," was never given to *deilia*. I used to envy him. He was always offering us words of encouragement: "Don't worry! God is good! The Lord will take care of things." More than once during the previous few months I'd had to borrow some of his courage because I didn't have enough of my own.

As I finally lifted my head from the table and pushed back my chair, the future loomed ahead of us like a wall of impenetrable fog. But over the years my brothers and I have learned a lot from Paul: "God did not give us a spirit of cowardice, but rather of power and love and self-control." The more we accepted the gift of that spirit from the Lord, the more confidently we could walk together toward whatever future the Lord had in mind for us.

Reflection

Think of something you are afraid of and consider how each of the three spirits mentioned in 2 Timothy might help you deal with that particular fear: (a) relying on God's power instead of your own; (b) loving (sharing your fear with others?); and (c) being rooted firmly in God.

Sacred Scripture

"Afraid" [*deilos*] or "fear" [*deilia*] appear in Wis 9:14; Sir 2:12; and 1 Macc 3:56.

Rule of Benedict

Do not be daunted immediately by fear and run away from the road that leads to salvation. It is bound to be narrow at the outset (Prologue v. 48).

3. Losing Your Nerve

"WHAT IF WE CAN'T GET ENOUGH STUDENTS to come?"

My own unsettling question jarred me out of a fretful half-sleep. I checked my alarm clock. Two A.M.

A month before, our monastic community had voted to reopen our inner-city school, St. Benedict's Prep. It was at best a chancy venture, but we assumed that the Lord would somehow take care of us. It was only when I lay awake at night that the problems started attacking in packs like monsters in a nightmare: "What if we can't raise enough money?; How can we run the thing if none of us has any experience in school administration?; What if God has other plans?" Of course I always believed that God would help us, but I also knew, without ever admitting it out loud, that our project was a very risky gamble and could easily fall apart.

I was caught between two contradictory beliefs—that the Lord would take care of us, and that the new school would fail before it ever began. Being caught in this position has, it seems, always been quite a common experience for Christians. I was happy to notice that it even happened to Saint Peter himself one night on the Sea of Galilee (Matthew 14:22–33). I learned a lot from his ordeal.

The apostles, you remember, were out on the sea in a boat in the middle of the night. Jesus, who had remained back on shore, suddenly appeared walking toward them on the water. They were frightened, thinking they were seeing a ghost. Peter, being his usual impulsive self, spoke up, "Lord, if it is you, tell me to come to you over the water," and Jesus invited him, "Come!" Peter immediately climbed out of the boat and began to walk on the water toward Jesus. So far so good. But when he saw how strong the wind was, Peter suddenly remembered that humans can't walk on water, and he became terrified. He started to sink, and shouted, "Lord, save me!" Immediately Jesus stretched out his hand, caught hold of Peter and lifted him to safety. Then the Lord scolded him, "O you of little faith! Why did you doubt" (Matthew 14:31)?

The Greek verb meaning "to doubt" is very revealing: *distazō*[7] comes from *di-*, "double" and *stasis*, "standing." Literally it means "to stand in two places at the same time." When Jesus asks Peter "Why did you doubt?" he is asking literally "Why were you standing in two places at once?" His question describes Peter's situation perfectly: Peter is thinking two contradictory things, namely that Jesus has the power to let someone walk on water, and that walking on water is physically impossible for humans, including him. *Distazō* also describes the struggle that was keeping me up at night. I was experiencing firsthand what the Prince of the Apostles must have felt when he tried to walk on the waves, when faith and doubt started wrestling with each other in his heart.

I had been drafting a school philosophy, designing a curriculum, and estimating a budget for the school in the belief that our idea would work. But there I was, unable to sleep, worried and wondering about the future. I firmly believed that God was in charge and would watch over us, but I also held on just as strongly to the idea that this project was liable to come crashing down around our ears. I kept switching back and forth between the two positions, and wound up standing in two places at once: Each evening, often exhausted with the effort of planning our new school, before getting into bed I would prayerfully leave the venture in God's hands, confident that the Almighty would take care of it, but then, in the middle of the night, I would lose my nerve and start to doubt that the Lord was really going to help. Standing spiritually in two places at once, I believed both things at the same time, and, just like poor Peter, I would panic. I would start to picture the catastrophe that was about to unfold, and begin tossing and turning, feeling alone, afraid and abandoned; then I would start to sink into the storm-tossed sea.

---

7. *Distazō* (dees-tad´-zo), "to doubt," from *di-*, "double" plus *stasis*, "standing;" literally: "stand in two places at the same time."

I untangled myself from the covers, which had gotten twisted by all my tossing and turning, and closed my eyes in one more attempt to get some sleep. I imagined myself and my brother Benedictines in an open boat that was being engulfed by towering waves in the middle of the night. Then I imagined Jesus walking toward us on the angry-looking waves. He looked a lot like a ghost. I said, "Lord, if it is you, tell me to come to you over the water." And he invited me, "Come!"

Just as I stepped out onto the water I finally fell asleep.

Reflection

1. When are you most likely to doubt God and "stand in two places?" When you are standing in two places, how does it feel? How do you act?

2. Using yet a different word for "doubt," James 1:6 reads: "Ask in faith, not doubting, for the one who doubts is like a wave of the sea that is driven and tossed about by the wind." Have you ever experienced being tossed around by the winds of doubt in a situation? If so, were you able to overcome those feelings eventually? If so, how?

Sacred Scripture

Distazō appears in an interesting context in Matt 28:17.

Another more common word for "doubt" also uses the root *di-*, "two." The adjective *dipsuchos,* "doubting, undecided," comes from *di-*, "double" + *psuche*, "heart, mind," and involves literally "being of two minds"; it is found in James 1:8 and 4:8.

Rule of Benedict

Place your hope in God alone (Chapter 4, "The Tools for Good Works," v. 41).

4. Being a Paraclete

THE SPRING SUNSHINE WAS BEAMING BRIGHTLY through the stained-glass windows of the church of Our Lady of the Most Blessed Sacrament, bathing the congregation and me in a multicolored glow—just right for Pentecost Sunday, 1972. I enjoyed exercising my ministry as a priest, celebrating mass here every Sunday, especially because this had been my parish church as a child. Sitting in the presider's chair on an elevated platform, I could see the entire church and all its familiar details: the wooden roof beams, the Stations of the Cross on the walls, the scenes in the stained-glass windows.

When the organ began playing the Offertory hymn, I started singing the familiar tune from memory, "Come Holy Ghost, Creator Blest. . . ." I was praying extra hard for the gift of the Spirit that morning because our monastic community was now actually writing out a curriculum for our proposed school, and I was the one in charge of putting together the course of studies. I swallowed hard at the thought, as I watched the ushers start to take up the collection using the same long-handled wicker baskets they used when I was sitting in those seats.

I studied the people in the pews. There were some familiar faces, most of them starting to show the passage of the years. I recognized one woman, though, who hadn't changed very much since my childhood; she had her six-year-old grandson beside her. I'd heard that she was raising him because his parents had gotten divorced and neither of them wanted the child. Then there were the more recent parishioners, African-Americans and folks from the Caribbean, many with children of different ages.

I was still singing the hymn from memory when we began the second verse "O Paraclete, to thee we cry. . . ." Oops! The congregation had just sung something different! What was it, "O Comforter, to thee we cry. . . ." The hymn continued, leaving me behind to think about the difference between calling on the Holy Spirit as "Comforter" instead of as "Paraclete."

Even if its meaning is pretty complex, the word "Paraclete" is rich with theological insight. It comes from *paraklētos*,[8] originally a legal term in classical Greek referring to someone literally "called to stand beside" an accused person and act as an ally and legal advisor.[9] As a result of these varied meanings, *paraklētos* offers many insights into how the Holy Spirit, the "Paraclete," works in our everyday lives. During his Last Supper discourses Jesus describes some of the roles of the Paraclete:[10] "The Paraclete, the Holy Spirit, whom the Father will send in my name, will teach you everything, and remind you of all that I have said to you" (John 14:26). "When the Paraclete comes, whom I will send to you from the Father, the Spirit of truth who comes from the Father, he will testify on my behalf" (John 15:26).

If Jesus is sending us the Paraclete to be a dynamic force in our lives, teaching, reminding, and witnessing, then the translation of *paraklētos* as "comforter" is a poor and misleading one. When John Wycliffe first translated it as "Comforter" in his English translation of the Bible in 1382, the verb "to comfort" still had its original Latin meaning based on the adjective *fortis*, "strong." It meant "to give strength," as a general might do for his troops before sending them into battle. Since then many translators have held on to Wycliffe's translation of *paraklētos* even though the meaning of the English "comforter" has changed radically. The Paraclete will come as "comforter" only in the original sense,

---

8. Parakaleō (par-ak-al-eh´-o) "to console, strengthen, encourage" comes from *para*, "beside" plus *kaleō* (kal-eh´-o), "to call."

9. It is used in this original sense of Jesus himself in the passage "But if anyone does sin, we have an Advocate [*paraklētos*] with the Father, Jesus Christ the righteous one" (1 John 2:1).

10. In the next two citations from John, the word "Paraclete" is translating *paraklētos*.

to give us courage and strengthen us for the struggles of life, to help us
to keep fighting our daily battles without losing heart.[11]

I was still thinking about the wonderful richness of "paraclete" as I
stood and began walking down the steps from the presider's chair and
past the altar to receive the gifts being brought in the Offertory procession that had already started towards me down the long center aisle.
As I walked I thought of a beautiful passage in which *paraklesis* is used
half a dozen times:[12] "Blessed be the God and Father of our Lord Jesus
Christ, the merciful Father and the God who gives us every possible
encouragement; he *supports* us in every hardship, so that we are able
to *come to the support of* others, in every hardship of theirs because of
the *encouragement* that we ourselves *receive* from God" (2 Corinthians
1:3–4). The point of the passage is clear: Since we have received the gift
of the Paraclete, the Lord is calling us to pass on that gift to others by
encouraging and helping our brothers and sisters who may need our
help. We are to be paracletes for one another.

As I stood waiting for the procession to arrive, I looked out over
the congregation as I usually did. To my left I noticed a woman whose
husband had died a few months before; sitting beside her, one on each
side, were her two longtime friends—they had now truly become paracletes for her, giving her strength and helping her through her ordeal.
In the pew behind them was the grandmother with her six-year old
grandson whom she was now raising—a grandmother turned paraclete. Just then the pastor, Father Denman, walked in the rear door of
the church. He was still good friends with my brother Bob from ten
years ago when Bob had been a member of the parish Catholic Youth
Organization. Fr. Denman had been a real help to so many young people over the years. And he'd now taken me, a young priest, under his

---

11. Paul uses a related word to tell the Romans, "Whatever was written previously
was written for our instruction, that by endurance and by the encouragement
[*paraklēsis*] of the scriptures we might have hope" (Romans 15:4).

12. Each italicized word in the following passage is a translation of the word
paraklēsis or the verb *parakaleō*.

wing, offering advice and sharing good ideas. Just this morning he'd given me my own copy of a little book for the Rite of Reconciliation. I thought to myself as I watched him walk down the side aisle, "He must truly enjoy being a paraclete."

Then I noticed Adele, who had come to me after mass a couple of months ago to introduce herself and invite me to drop by for Sunday dinner to meet her husband and her several children. That had been just at the time when we were beginning to think seriously about starting some sort of "new" school. As it had turned out, her husband, Carl, a successful businessman, had in the space of two months become our community's most important paraclete, attending meetings to offer his encouragement and practical ideas. He had certainly been an important help to me personally in my moments of doubt and fear. Last week, in a dramatic vote of confidence, he had enrolled his son Tim as one of the first students in our non-existent school. "Now that's a paraclete," I said to myself as the procession arrived and I started accepting the gifts of bread and wine.

As I turned around to carry the gifts to the altar, which was now glowing with Pentecost light from the windows, it occurred to me that the Holy Spirit was certainly present in our congregation that Pentecost morning—the place was full of paracletes.

Reflection

1. Which translation of *paraklētos* best conveys what God has been for you lately: Helper, Encourager, Strengthener, or Consoler? Reflect on some ways in which God plays, has played, or could play that role for you.

2. The passage from 2 Cor 1:3–4 cited on the previous page says that we have been given the Spirit so that we can be of service to others in need. When have you acted as a paraclete for someone by your support or encouragement?

3. Think of a few times when someone served as a paraclete for you.

Sacred Scripture

1. The noun *paraklētos* appears in John 14:16 and 15:26.
2. The noun *paraklēsis* appears in Luke 2:25 (where Simeon was awaiting the "consolation" of Israel).
3. The verb *parakaleō* appears in Luke 3:18; Acts 16:40; and 1 Thess 4:18. It is the verb in the beatitude, "Blest are they who mourn, for they will be comforted [*parakaleō*]" (Matt 5:4).

Rule of Benedict

You must relieve the lot of the poor, clothe the naked, visit the sick, and bury the dead. Go to help the troubled and console the sorrowing (Chapter 4, "The Tools for Good Works," vv. 14–19).

CHAPTER TWO

LEARNING TO LET GO

Knee Surgery

One freezing December afternoon in 1980 I was playing on the faculty team during the annual student-faculty touch football game at the "new" St. Benedict's, now in its eighth year. During the course of the game, as I was running full-tilt across the frozen field my left foot slipped, causing my leg to whip out behind me. The pain in my knee made me scream as I fell to the ground, praying that the agony wouldn't make me pass out. I had completely torn the anterior cruciate ligament in my left knee, and would have to spend part of Christmas vacation in the hospital undergoing surgery to repair it.

This painful experience forced me to admit that at thirty-eight I was no longer young. In addition, the eleven wearisome weeks I spent on crutches gave me plenty of time to absorb a number of other valuable lessons about such things as patience, love, ambition, and depending on others. The following reflections deal with four of those discoveries.

5. Weaving the Web of Love

I WAS PLAYING DEFENSIVE END FOR THE FACULTY in the annual student-faculty touch football game. A December cold snap had left the grass of the football field frozen. I could hear it crunch under my feet as I sprinted to head off a speedy sophomore named Vernon, who was trying to turn the corner and run down the sideline with the ball. To this day I believe I would have caught him if my left foot hadn't slipped on the treacherous, icy grass. My leg snapped out behind me like a whip and the next thing I knew I was rolling on the field clutching my knee, my vision blurred with the horrible pain of a dislocated kneecap and a torn ligament. After a few agonizing seconds my kneecap went back into place and I opened my eyes to look up into a circle of concerned and curious faces peering down at me. I heard a familiar voice trying to calm me with reassuring words about my being all right.

"Can you walk?" a second voice asked me as a couple of my teammates began lifting me carefully to my feet. I found that I couldn't put any weight on the bad leg, but could hobble along if I leaned on someone.

I limped off the field with my left arm draped over the shoulders of Jack, our head basketball coach, who had taught me freshman history twenty-four years before. I could still picture him behind his teacher's desk in that classroom. As the two of us worked our way slowly to the locker room, I thought of all the many ways I was connected to people around here: to my brothers in the monastery, to my students, to my fellow teachers—and even to a couple of my former teachers.

One time I was at a meeting in a nearby parish when someone began being extremely critical of a person who was not present. A woman from Ghana broke in on the critic to warn her to be careful about speaking ill of others. "Back home in my village we have a saying:

'People are like pumpkins in a field; we are all interconnected by vines, but there are so many vines and they are so intertwined that you can't tell who is related to who.' So if you speak ill of someone in the next village, that person might turn out to be a distant relative of yours. And then you would be disgraced."

Ever since that evening, I've prized that saying not as a proverb about complex tribal genealogies but as a down-to-earth image of the unseen web of countless interconnections and relationships of love that link all of us to one another.

Over the next fourteen weeks of casts and crutches, I was to see that network of love in action: students would hold doors and carry my books for me, my brothers in the monastery would go out of their way to do little tasks that I couldn't do for myself and offer to drive me to the doctor's, and various relatives and friends would call to offer their help or to ask how I was doing. When I thanked one cousin for being such a real help to me she said, "Hey, this is what it's supposed to be all about, isn't it?"

In the gospels our Lord doesn't talk about pumpkin fields, but rather about grapevines. John gives to the image of the vine tremendous power and depth by combining it with one of his favorite words, the verb, *menō*,[1] "to dwell, to remain." He uses it in the last supper discourses to describe the deep, intimate, mutual indwelling that binds Jesus with the Father who dwells in him (John 14:10). No other word captures better the mystery and intensity of Jesus' relationship with his Father. Later on

---

1. *Menō* (men´-o), to remain physically in one place, and (figuratively) to last over a period of time. The word is used some 38 times in the Fourth Gospel, triple the number in the other three gospels combined.

Jesus expands the scope of the verb to include not just the Father and himself but also his apostles, inviting them to share in the deep, mysterious, intimate life of the Trinity itself. At one point in his discourse to his disciples at the last supper he uses *menō* ten times in seven verses:[2]

> *Remain* in me, as I remain in you. Just as a branch cannot bear fruit on its own unless it *remains* on the vine, so neither can you unless you *remain* in me. I am the vine, you are the branches. Whoever *remains* in me and I in him will bear much fruit. . . . *Remain* in my love. If you keep my commandments, you will *remain* in my love, just as I have kept my Father's commandments and *remain* in his love. (John 15:1–10 *passim*, NAB)

Now, with this speech Jesus has included his apostles and all future believers in the vine of divine love that had begun with him, his Father, and the Holy Spirit.

But the image evoked by *menō*—the divine, mutual indwelling of the Father and the Son, the dwelling of Christ in the Christian, and the dwelling of the Christian in Christ—is not about merely hanging around together in some staid, static relationship in which nothing happens. Rather, divine indwelling involves vibrant activity. For John the universe was created by love and is kept in existence by the vital, all-encompassing Spirit of love that unites the Father, the Son, all of humanity, and indeed the entire universe. Love takes on human form every time we "are there" for a brother or sister to bring someone through a time of pain or discouragement—or to carry their books or drive them to the doctor's office.

Finally Jack and I reached the locker room where I let go of his shoulder and lowered myself gingerly onto a bench. I didn't know as I sat there that I was about to begin three months on crutches. Nor did I suspect that as the long weeks wore on, the care and concern of so many people would make me so aware of how interconnected we all are in the network of love.

---

2. Each of the italicized words in the following excerpt translates the verb *menō*.

Looking back now, I realize that, because I experienced how good it felt to have someone do a simple favor for me when I was on crutches, I would become much more aware when someone around me needed someone to hold a door open for them or carry something up a flight of stairs. I found, too, that passing the love along to others was another way of experiencing the meaning of that beautiful verb *menō*, the fact that we are all connected with one another, with God, and with the universe in an infinite, mysterious, mutual indwelling love.

I still see the love continuing to grow quietly each day, connecting us like a wonderful lush vine that reaches around the world into homes and hospitals, offices and factories, classrooms and shopping malls— and even across frozen football fields.

Reflection

1. Reread slowly the shortened version of John 15:4–10 that appears on the previous page, watching for the various intimate, inward connections expressed by *menō*.

2. When do you feel most connected with Christ, the vine? What is the "fruit" that you bear when you are connected to Christ? How can you strengthen the web of love in the world?

3. What can make you feel cut off or disconnected from the vine? Think of some steps you might take to stay more closely connected to Jesus and to the network of love he came to give us.

Sacred Scripture

Menō meaning "stay" is found in Luke 1:56 and Acts 18:3; *menō* as "endure over time" is used in John 6:27 and 1 John 2:17.

Rule of Benedict

This, then, is the good zeal which monks must foster with fervent love: They should each try to be the first to show respect to the other, supporting with the greatest patience one another's weaknesses of body or behavior (Chapter 72, "The Good Zeal of Monks," vv. 3–5).

6. Leaning on the Lord

I WAS SPENDING CHRISTMAS MORNING in the hospital in a Demerol-induced fog, my throbbing left knee wrapped in Ace bandages after surgery on my torn anterior cruciate ligament. I was staring absently at the tan rubber drain coming out of my bandaged knee when there was a gentle knock on the door. I whispered hoarsely "Come in!" and was surprised to see a man, a woman, and two children walking slowly into my room and wishing me a Merry Christmas. They introduced themselves and said that they had been coming to the hospital on Christmas morning for years to sing carols in patients' rooms. I managed a weak smile and a thank you.

As they began to sing I couldn't wait for them to leave—which made me feel ashamed for being so ungrateful to these good-hearted people who were being so kind and loving to me, a stranger. They made me feel uncomfortable, and not just because the Demerol was starting to wear off. No, there was something else going on.

It was only after they had finished their three carols and had left that I realized why their visit had been so unpleasant for me: I had been uncomfortable with being on the receiving end. As a priest, I was used to always being the giver: I gave homilies, distributed communion, offered blessings, and gave absolution in confession. As a teacher, too, I was a professional giver of lessons, homework, grades, and advice. Heck, come to think of it, I'd even played my guitar and sung for people in their hospital rooms. But, now that I was on the receiving end, it was taking some getting used to. I had to accept that relatives and friends were going out of their way to come to visit me, that others were bringing me my meals and medicine, and people I didn't even know had just given up their Christmas morning to come and sing me carols. I had certainly been forced out of my usual role of "helper."

A few minutes after the singers left, I wanted to use the bathroom. The surgeon had said that I was allowed to, but getting out of bed was a challenge—especially because it required asking someone to help me. I rang the buzzer. Since I didn't have a cast yet, the slightest bending of my bad knee would send sharp, stabbing pains up my leg. So if I wanted to swing my knees over the side of the bed, someone would have to hold my left leg perfectly straight for me. After a few minutes, a nurse came into the room, wishing me a Merry Christmas and asking how I was. Not wanting to spoil her Christmas, the helper inside of me lied and said I felt great. Then I asked her if she could help me get out of bed to use the bathroom.

"Sure. Let's go. But take your time and be careful."

She didn't need to tell *me* to be careful. I wanted to tell *her* to be careful! But she seemed to know from experience that she had to lift up on my heel so as to keep the knee from bending as I swung my leg over the side of the bed.

"Slide over more towards your right . . . That's it . . . Okay now very slowly, swing your legs over the side and I'll hold your heel to keep your knee from bending . . . Ready?"

I watched as she gently and confidently took my heel in her expert hands, then I focused on her kind face as I started to swing my knees across the bed. I wondered when she would celebrate Christmas with her family. "Good; okay," she said. "That's it. Keep coming now. Slowly . . . slowly." I was holding my breath, waiting for the stabs of pain. But she obviously knew how important it was not to let that knee bend. "Okay. Almost there," she announced. She kept a firm hold on my heel, keeping the knee straight as I lowered both feet toward to floor. Then I shifted my weight a little. Bad move.

"Yow!" I gasped, "Ow!" I actually saw bright flashes of pain for a second or two. "Sorry!" she apologized, sympathetic but unfazed. "Okay, we're just about there. You're fine . . . There we are. Good job!"

I breathed a deep sigh as I rested my two feet on the floor, beads of clammy perspiration starting to form on my forehead. She was right, though, the hard part was over. I took a deep breath and raised myself carefully onto the crutches that she held out for me. As I stood there leaning on my crutches, trying to slow my racing heartbeat, I realized what a powerful lesson I'd just had: For the first time that I could remember, I, the professional helper, had given myself completely, trustingly, and quite literally into the hands of someone else!

The role reversal was challenging. But it had a sort of biblical ring to it: "into your hands. . . ." The Bible is always challenging us to trust more in God. But we find out that trusting God requires not only courage but also a single-mindedness that keeps us from placing our trust in other things instead. A while back I came across a helpful New Testament word that put that Christmas morning experience into perspective.

The Greek verb *peithō*, "to trust in, to rely on"[3] highlights some of the challenges that people have in trying to trust in God alone. Some people, for example, put their trust instead in material possessions (Psalms 49:6–7), and others in the temple and religious practices (Jeremiah 7:3–8).[4]

Under the nurse's watchful eye I hobbled carefully across the floor, leaning on my crutches. I smiled when I remembered that Paul says that his sufferings in Asia had taught him to rely on God: "for we were so utterly, unbearably crushed that we despaired of life itself. Indeed, we felt that we had received the sentence of death so that we would rely [*peithō*] not on ourselves but on God who raises the dead" (2 Corinthians 1:8–9). I saw that I was in the middle of learning the same thing Paul had learned, namely that suffering can teach you that you can't rely simply on yourself.[5]

---

3. *Peithō* (pī´-tho) has many meanings, among which are "to rely on, to have confidence, to trust." It is used by Luke in its ordinary sense: "When a strong man fully armed guards his palace, his possessions are safe. But when one stronger than he attacks and overcomes him, he takes away the armor on which he relied [peithō] and distributes the spoils" (Luke 11:21–22).

4. In Phil 3:2 Paul warns against Jewish converts who "rely on" circumcision for salvation instead of on Christ.

5. Luke tells us that Jesus addressed the parable of "the Pharisee and the Tax Collector" to "those who *trust in* themselves that they are righteous and despise the rest" (Luke 18:9).

Arriving at the bathroom I leaned my shoulder for a moment against the door jamb because I was getting lightheaded with the effort. I could tell that I was in for a long, humbling, uncomfortable, and even painful learning experience.

Many times since then I've had occasion to put my trust completely in the Lord; and sometimes, as I've placed myself in God's hands, I've remembered vividly that Christmas morning in St. Mary's hospital when the kind nurse said, "Okay, swing your legs over the side and I'll hold your heel to keep your knee from bending . . . Ready?"

Reflection

1. Can you think of someone you know personally who seems able to trust wholeheartedly in the Lord?

2. Slowly read Matthew's account of the crucifixion (Matthew 27:36–50). Some of the bystanders taunt Jesus with the prophetic remark, "He trusted [*peithō*] in the Lord, let him deliver him now, if he wants to" (Matthew 27:43). They are quoting Psalm 22, verse 9: "He trusted in the Lord, let him deliver him. . . ." Reflect on Jesus' total self-abandonment to the Father; he has nothing left to hold on to: no material possessions, no religious rituals, no self-satisfied virtue, no accomplishments—nothing but God. Think of some situation in your life where God may be asking you to abandon yourself into the Father's hands.

Sacred Scripture

Peithō, "to trust" is used a few times in the psalms: Ps 2:11; Ps 25:1–2; Ps 118:8; and Ps 125:1.

Rule of Benedict

[The monk] shall imitate by his actions that saying of the Lord: I have come not to do my own will, but the will of him who sent me (Chapter 7, "Humility," v. 32).

7. Seeking God

I WAS SLUMPED IN MY ARMCHAIR in my room in the monastery. Beside me, leaning against the wall, were the crutches that I would need for the next eleven weeks. While I had been in the hospital, workers had sandblasted the exterior of the monastery, causing a fine gritty dust to filter into all the rooms. I stared helplessly at the disaster around me: everything was covered with grit—windowsills, floor, desk, books, everything. And there I sat with my leg immobilized in my new bulky cast, completely unable to do anything about the mess around me. Opening a door was a major challenge, getting to the bathroom down the hall was a project, and sweeping my floor an impossibility. I felt life starting to overwhelm me.

Suddenly my eyes filled with tears and I pounded the arms of my chair. "Damn! How am I supposed to get anything done? How am I supposed to get around? What about all the work I'm supposed to be doing?"

Frustration quickly turned to anger: "Fine! Then I'm just going to sit here and not do a thing! I'll just be like one of those crippled beggars in the gospel sitting at the side of the road!"

Wincing, I shifted my weight, trying to find a more comfortable position for my aching knee. Then I just sat still for a while feeling sorry for myself, doing my crippled beggar routine.

Soon, though, despite my dark mood, and because I couldn't really do anything else, I began to smile at my comical exaggeration of my woes, and admitted that maybe I was getting a bit melodramatic. Little by little, helpless and confined to my chair in my grit-covered room, I began to see things differently. The lesson started to sink in: There were other ways of living besides constantly running around and doing things.

It occurred to me that I had always been very good at organizing projects and bringing them to completion. I got a real sense of satisfaction from my hard work in our school, where I usually accomplished whatever goals I'd set. I started to realize, however, I tended to reduce most things in life to projects, even my relationship with the Lord, which I thought of as my monastic project of seeking God.

The Rule of Benedict says that the main thing to find out about someone applying for admission into the monastery is "if he truly seeks God." In fact, "seeking the Lord" is actually a familiar part of the Christian spiritual tradition. The idea of chasing around after the Lord is really attractive to people like me who run around too much anyway and who love pursuing and accomplishing goals. The New Testament is filled with people seeking Jesus: Herod searches for the infant Jesus,[6] Joseph and Mary look for him in Jerusalem when he is twelve,[7] and Simon and the disciples tell Jesus "Everyone is looking for you."[8]

But as I sat there glowering at my useless left leg, which looked like a pale yellow log wrapped in molded fiberglass mesh, I found it hard to picture myself chasing after anything—including God. I began to suspect that something crucial was missing from my conveniently one-sided image of seeking God.

Then it struck me that it's just as true to say that God is constantly seeking me! I began to picture myself not as a crippled beggar on the side of the road, but as the tax collector Zacchaeus perched on a tree branch. He was a successful and competent man who one day made a project out of seeking God.

The story, as you know, is that as Jesus was passing through Jericho, a wealthy tax collector named Zacchaeus wanted to see him, but being short, Zacchaeus had to climb into a tree to catch even a glimpse of him. When Jesus spotted him up there he called to him, "Zacchaeus, come down. I must dine with you today." With that sentence the initiative switched from the tax collector to Jesus. The tables were completely

---

6. Matthew 2:13.

7. Luke 2:48, 49.

8. Mark 1:37.

turned, and Zacchaeus's project of seeking Jesus was forgotten. The story had begun with Zacchaeus seeking to see Jesus, but now Jesus was seeking him.

Luke points up this reversal with a clever wordplay based on the word *zēteō*, "to seek:"[9] At the beginning of the story Zacchaeus was "seeking [*zēteō*][10] to see who Jesus was" and so climbed into a tree. But at the end of the story when pious people complained that Jesus was eating in the house of a sinner, the Lord answered them, "Today salvation has come to this house because this man too is a descendant of Abraham. For the Son of Man has come to seek [*zēteō*] and to save what was lost" (Luke 19:9–10). Here is the verb *zēteō*[11] again. This time, however, it is not Zacchaeus but the Lord who is doing the seeking. The story started with Zacchaeus seeking Jesus, but it ended with his finding out that all along it was Jesus who had come seeking *him*.

While it may look as if Christ was eating at Zacchaeus's table, the play on the verb points to a deeper reality: Zacchaeus was now eating at Jesus' table, being nurtured by the intimacy of God's forgiving love. Jesus had successfully sought out the seeker.

I shifted in my chair again. "Ouch! That hurt! I have to learn how to sit still. Humph! That should be interesting."

The story of Zacchaeus teaches us that no matter who we are, whether a monk whose vocation is to "truly seek God" in the monastery, or a layperson seeking to find God in everyday life, our spirituality cannot be based solely on chasing around after the Lord. For all of our impassioned, ceaseless effort of seeking God, it is ultimately God who is searching for us in hundreds of ways, but especially in people who love us.

---

9. *Zēteō* (dzay-teh´-o), 1. "to seek, look for," 2. "to attempt, seek to do something."

10. This is the verb *zēteō* meaning "to attempt," as when "some men brought on a stretcher a man who was paralyzed; they were trying [*zēteō*] to bring him in and set him in his presence" (Matthew 13:46).

11. This is *zēteō* meaning "to seek out," as when Jesus asks what the good shepherd would do: "Will he not leave the ninety-nine in the hills and go in search of [*zēteō*] the stray" (Matthew 18:12)?

Still feeling miserable and overwhelmed, I didn't feel in any shape to be climbing onto a tree branch. But my dusty chair, I figured, would serve the purpose quite well. I would just have to keep sitting here, like Zacchaeus on his branch, and not lose heart; I would have to believe that Jesus would catch up with me in his own good time.

I started to relax as I began to sense that the Lord was already close by, looking for me.

For Reflection

1. What does it mean for you to "seek God?" Does this seeking change in times of trial?

2. Have you ever had the feeling that God was pursuing you but you were running away? If so, what did you do when you realized that you were avoiding God?

3. Sit and pray quietly, imagining yourself to be Zacchaeus sitting on his tree branch waiting for the Lord to come by. How does this feel?

Sacred Scripture

All of the following passages contain *zēteō*, and each is well worth meditating on: 1 Chr 16:10–11; Ps 27:8; Matt 6:33, 7:7, 18:12; Luke 24:5; and John 5:30.

Rule of Benedict

The concern must be whether the novice truly seeks God (Chapter 58, "The Procedure for Receiving Brothers," v. 7).

Seeking his workman in a multitude of people, the Lord calls out to him and lifts his voice again: is there anyone here who yearns for life and desires to see good days? (Prologue v. 14).

8. A Work in Progress

"Seven . . . eight . . . nine . . . ten! Ouf!"

Lying on my back in gym shorts and a tee shirt, I tried to lower my foot gently onto the exercise mat so that the five-pound exercise boot wouldn't dent the floor of my room in the monastery. Then taking a deep breath I began the last set of straight-knee leg raises.

"One . . . two . . . three . . . four . . ."

The surgeon had given me two pages of daily exercises for rehabilitating my knee. This was going to be a long process.

A few months before this as I hobbled off the touch football field, I had said good-by to my left anterior cruciate ligament and to the image of myself as "young." At the age of thirty-eight I'd had to face the undeniable fact that I was no longer able to do all the things I used to do as a teenager.

"Five . . . six . . . seven . . ."

But lying there that afternoon I saw that this knee injury had put to the test something that some wise friends had already been teaching me: that it was okay to be imperfect, and that people managed to love one another despite everyone's faults, foibles, and imperfections. Well, for the past several weeks people around me had been putting up with my crutches and cast, with my inability to carry anything in my hands, or even drive myself to the doctor's. I had to admit that so far my being terribly imperfect had not seemed to make anyone run away in horror. In fact a lot of folks had been going out of their way to be of help to me.

Realizing that it is okay to be imperfect had some good side effects. For one thing, I no longer had to waste energy and effort trying to hide the fact that I was imperfect. And secondly, if it was okay for me to be imperfect, then that meant it was okay for everyone else to be imperfect, too—an idea that would definitely make me a more patient teacher and a better community member, not to mention a wiser Novice Master.

"Eight . . . nine . . . ten! Ouf!"

Not many months before hurting my knee I had finally concluded one last piece of unfinished business that had been nagging me for some time. It was that troublesome command of Jesus, "You must be perfect—just as your heavenly father is perfect"(Matthew 5:48). I had finally come to admit that I did not need to be perfect, and I also knew that only God was perfect. So Jesus couldn't have been asking me to be perfect. Fine, that was what he had *not* meant; but then just what *had* he meant by his curious command?

I undid the straps on the metal "boot" and then turned and lay on my right side. Carefully following the directions on the paper given me by the surgeon, I slowly brought my leg forward, parallel to the floor, in a kicking motion, trying to keep the knee straight. I stretched it as far as I could and then let my foot rest on the floor. "Now count to ten. . . . Ready? . . . One . . . two . . . three . . ."

Despite the fact that Jesus' command to "be perfect" was so odd, it was a surprisingly long time before I thought to look up this confusing command in the original language. The very first time I read the Greek, though, I saw right where the problem lay: with the adjective *teleios* that was being translated as "perfect." *Teleios*, you see, is based on the noun *telos*, "an end or goal," and so actually it means "having attained its end or purpose, complete."[12] Often in the New Testament it simply means "mature" as opposed to "immature," as it does, say, in the verse "You need milk, not solid food . . . solid food is for the mature [*teleios*]" (Hebrews 5:12–14).

Teleios has a dynamic feel and suggests a process of growth and development, of striving toward the goal (*telos*) of fullness and moral maturity. In any case there's nothing here about a frozen state of "perfection."

---

12. The noun *telos* (tel´os), "goal," is the basis for several words: the adjective *teleios* (tel´-ee-os), "perfect, fully developed," the verbs *teleō* and *teleioō* meaning to bring to completion, to end, and the noun *teleia*, "perfection, completeness."

"Eight . . . nine . . . ten." Now I had to slowly bring the leg back, keeping my knee straight. The final piece of the puzzle had come when I looked at the verses immediately preceding this sentence in the Sermon on the Mount. Evidently many Jews at the time of Christ had been ignoring the precepts laid down in Exodus concerning obligations toward foreigners and enemies[13] and had narrowed their interpretation of the command, "love your neighbor," to include only their fellow Jews, and surely not their enemies. In the Sermon in the Mount, Jesus challenges their way of thinking:

> You have heard that it was said, "You shall love your neighbor and hate your enemy." But I say to you, Love your enemies and pray for those who persecute you, so that you may be children of your Father in heaven; for he makes his sun rise on the evil and on the good, and sends rain on the righteous and on the unrighteous. (Matthew 5:43–45)

The heavenly Father, instead of setting limits on divine love, "makes his sun rise on the bad and the good, and causes rain to fall on the just and the unjust," and our love must imitate God's way of loving. It is at this point that Matthew concludes with a summarizing sentence, the notorious "Be perfect, therefore, as your heavenly Father is perfect."

The command "Be *teleios* as your heavenly Father is *teleios*" urges us to keep striving to achieve our innate goal of being conformed to the image of God in us, a God who loves everyone with no limits and no conditions. *The New Jerusalem Bible's* free translation of the command captures this point nicely: "You must set no bounds on your love just as your Father who is in heaven sets no bounds on his love" (Matthew 5:48 NJB).

---

13. One example is this: "When you come upon your enemy's ox or donkey going astray, you shall bring it back. When you see the donkey of one who hates you lying under its burden and you would hold back from setting it free, you must help to set it free. You shall not oppress a resident alien; you know the heart of an alien, for you were aliens in the land of Egypt" (Exodus 23: 4–5, 9).

The command to set no bounds on our love may be very challenging, but it is neither impossible nor discouraging. It calls us to keep on striving and growing, along with all of our imperfect brothers and sisters until that day when we all attain "the full stature of Christ" in heaven. It calls us to think of ourselves as works in progress and to be patient with others who are likewise works in progress. It challenges us to keep striving to be fully ourselves by learning to love as God loves—without boundaries. The fact that we are sometimes not very good at it simply shows that we are not yet in heaven, where all of us will one day be perfected. But God is not finished with us yet; and that's okay. God loves us, just as our friends do, even when we're not perfect.

Still lying on my right side, I slowly brought my leg forward again in a kicking motion, careful to keep the knee straight. I stretched it out as far as I could and then rested my foot on the floor. Then I counted to ten again: "One . . . two . . . three . . ."

A quick glance at my injured knee told me, if I had any doubts, that I was certainly not perfect; and these exercises would be reminding me for the next four months that I was definitely a work in progress.

Reflection

1. How do you react to being a work in progress? Does it make you feel good? Disappointed? Impatient? Do you find it easier to put up with other people's imperfections or with your own?

2. The idea that even the church is a work in progress is expressed in the Letter to the Ephesians: "We should grow in every way into him who is the head, Christ . . . building up the body of Christ until we attain to full maturity (literally "to the mature [*teleios*] man") to the extent of the full stature of Christ" (Eph 4:11–15). How do you react to the church's imperfections, especially ones that affect you directly or that are pounced on by the news media?

Sacred Scripture

Teleios appears in these passages: Matt 19:21; Rom 12:2; 1 Cor 2:6, 13:10, 14:20; Phil 3:15; Col 1:28; and 1 John 4:18.

Wisdom of the Desert

One of the brethren had sinned, and the priest told him to leave the community. So then Abba Bessarion got up and walked out with him, saying: I too am a sinner![14]

---

14. Thomas Merton, *The Wisdom of the Desert* (New York, New Directions, 1970), 40.

CHAPTER THREE

GETTING HOLLOWED OUT
The Death of My Brother Bob

I grew up in a family with two older brothers and a younger sister. The one I was closest to was my brother Bob, just sixteen months older than me. As youngsters we were inseparable, playing together, sharing confidences and ideas, and quarrelling the way close siblings do. Even after I joined the monastery, Bob continued to be my close friend and a dependable support.

He had been suffering from mysterious back pain for some months when suddenly one December night in 1986, at the age of forty-five, he became terribly weak and dizzy. He was rushed to the hospital where tests showed that he was riddled with lymphoma. Although he battled bravely for several long, painful months, the cancer relentlessly wasted his body until it eventually took his life in early June. Bob left behind his wife and four young children.

His death overwhelmed me, devastated me, and plunged me into a grief too deep for words. It shook the foundation of my faith and put to the test my most basic assumptions: that life makes sense, for example, or that God is infinitely kind, or that I need to be in perfect control of my emotions. To be honest, ever since that experience I've never been quite the same—but then, I've come to realize, maybe that was the idea: I wasn't supposed to be the same.

Over the years since then I've come to realize that through this mysterious catastrophe, God has done some tremendous life-giving things in many people, including me. The next four meditations suggest a few of the many lessons I've drawn from the most tragic period in my life.

9. Reading with the Eyes of Faith

WHEN I STEPPED QUIETLY INTO THE HOSPITAL ROOM I found my brother propped up on some pillows in the bed near the door, looking pale and exhausted. For the past two weeks I had been visiting him in the ICU amid blinking monitors and a ventilator machine pumping air into his lungs through a tube inserted at the base of his throat. As his wife and children and the rest of us watched and worried about his slow progress, the wearying days wore on. To make things even harder, the "trache" tube in his throat hadn't allowed him to speak, so he'd had to laboriously write everything onto a little pad—an arrangement that didn't encourage a lot of small talk.

That morning I'd gotten a call from his wife, Judy, that he had finally been moved from the ICU into a regular room and that the breathing tube had been removed. Knowing that he would now be able to speak, I had driven to the hospital looking forward to our first conversation since the start of this whole ordeal. When I walked into his room he gave me a weary but warm smile, and in a voice made gravelly by the recently removed breathing tube he whispered, "Hi!"

I took his hand and looked into his tired eyes. "How are you?" I asked.

"Okay. Better," he whispered hoarsely.

Then quite spontaneously I asked, "Well, what's the story? Have you figured out what God's been up to?"

His answer came back right away, as if he'd been thinking about nothing else for the past two weeks; he whispered with complete conviction, "Al, he's rebuilding me!"

For a moment I stood speechless, marveling at the deep wisdom of his answer. But I wasn't completely surprised either; he had always been a thoughtful and spiritual person. As we continued talking I started to realize that he was looking at his suffering so completely with the eyes of faith that he was able to peer deeply into the mysterious meaning of his illness. And I, the monk and priest, unable to see it that way, was helplessly shattered by it all. He was able to see that as his body was wasting away, a deeper and opposite process was taking place: He had realized that God was rebuilding him by means of the suffering.

I had certainly learned a few things about God's strange ways when St. Benedict's closed fourteen years earlier, and when I'd spent eleven weeks on crutches after my knee operation in 1980. But Bob's view of his illness showed me that my view of life was still pretty shallow compared to his. Just how shallow I would find out a month later, when he died.

My grief over Bob's death was far deeper than I could ever have imagined. The enormous, inexplicable, wordless pain made me understand for the first time the real meaning of the word "grief." Probably what made the pain worse than anything I'd ever felt before was that I wasn't able to see with Bob's eyes of faith. All I saw was that my brother and best friend had died of a wasting disease, leaving a widow and four young children.

It took months of crying and anger and deep, deep sadness before I started to catch little glimpses of how Bob had seen things. One of the first of these insights came half a year later around Christmas 1987 as I was reading Luke's narrative of Jesus' birth. The Christmas story was so familiar that I could read it easily in the Greek, which is what I was doing one morning when suddenly Bob gave me a Christmas present, a little piece of his vision.

It started when I came across one of my favorite words, the noun *rhēma*, "word."[1] What had always fascinated me about *rhēma* was that it had come to mean not just "word," but also what the word referred to; and so it could also mean "thing, object, matter, event."[2]

---

1. *Rhēma* (hray´-mah), "1. utterance, word, 2. event, thing;" plural, *rhēmata*. Pilate asks Jesus, " 'Do you not hear how many things they are testifying against you?' But [Jesus] did not answer him one word" [*rhēma*] (Matthew 27:14).

2. Saint Paul, for example, writes that "On the testimony of two or three witnesses a fact [*rhēma*] shall be established" (2 Corinthians 13:1).

As I read further in Luke's Christmas story, I enjoyed watching him play with the two different meanings of *rhēma*, "word" and "event." After the mysterious events surrounding the birth of John the Baptist, "fear came upon all the neighbors, and all these things [*rhēmata*] were discussed throughout the hill country of Judea." On Christmas, the shepherds said to one another, "Let us go, then, to Bethlehem to see this thing [*rhēma*] that has taken place." Arriving at the stable "they made known the message [*rhēma*] that had been told them about this child. . . . And Mary kept all these things [*rhēmata*], reflecting on them in her heart" (Luke 1:64–2:19 *passim*).[3]

The shepherds went to see the *rhēma* that had taken place, and Mary kept all these *rhēmata* in her heart; these were not "words" but "events." Suddenly I began to catch a glimpse of a crucial truth that Bob had seen so clearly. Luke, by playing on the double meaning of "word" and "event," was inviting us to see the birth of Jesus on two levels. First, there was the visible, historical *event* in time and space: a baby boy had been born in a small town (or a man had died of lymphoma in a large hospital). Second, for a person of faith that event was also a *word* that by its nature stood for something else, pointing beyond itself to some meaning. The essential question to ask about any word was after all, "What does it mean?"

As I kept reflecting on this double meaning of "word" and "event," I began to understand a little better what I had seen in that hospital room months before. While Bob was lying for long hours in the ICU,

---

3. Years later, after Mary and Joseph found the twelve-year-old Jesus in the temple and brought him home with them, "his mother kept all these things [*rhēmata*] in her heart" (Luke 2:51).

he had been doing exactly what Mary used to do, quietly consulting his heart and trying to "read" an event as if it were a word that conveyed a meaning. She had pondered the mysterious words of the angel Gabriel (see Luke 1:29), reflected on the meaning of the visit of the three wise men (Matthew 2:9–12), and meditated on the somber prophecy of Simeon (Luke 2:25–35), searching each time for what the Almighty might be asking of her. Bob had reflected on the "event" of his terrible ordeal with lymphoma, and had seen in it a "word" from God, while I could see only a tragic event.

The first Christmas without Bob was painful, as anyone would know who has ever celebrated that first holiday after the death of a loved one. But the pain was eased a little bit by the glimmer of light shed by my friend *rhēma* in the Christmas readings, assuring me that sooner or later I, too, would be able to read the terrible "event" of Bob's death as a "word" that made at least a little sense.

And indeed, in the following months and years I would come to share more and more of Bob's vision, and would start to see some meaning in the events surrounding his death. I discovered, for example, that by hollowing me out they had made a little more room in my heart for other people and for God. I discovered, too, that my grieving had given me a special bond with others who were being overwhelmed by grief the way I had been.

As time goes on I still miss Bob, but I also occasionally see some new gift that has come from that horrible event; I can look at the *rhēma* of his death and read it a little more clearly as a word from the Lord.

But that afternoon as I left his hospital room depressed and miserable, I wasn't able to read anything. Not one single word.

Reflection

1. Think of an event that eventually became a "word" for you. What was its meaning for you? How did you arrive at the meaning? Did it take a long time for you to understand it?

2. Are there certain kinds of events that you find easier to "read" than others? If so, what is it that makes some more difficult to understand?

Sacred Scripture

Rhēma is translated as "word" in Matt 12:36; Acts 6:11; and Heb 11:3. The same noun is translated as "subject, thing, event" in Acts 5:32 and 13:42.

Rule of Benedict

Never swerving from his instructions, then, but faithfully observing his teaching in the monastery until death, we shall through patience share in the sufferings of Christ that we may deserve also to share in his kingdom. Amen (Prologue, v. 50).

10. The Healing Visit

"HI, PHYLLIS!" I greeted the nurse, "How's Bob today?"

I had stopped at the nurses' station on my way to my brother's room to find out how he was doing that afternoon.

"He was a little better this morning," she answered, looking up from a patient's chart. "The doctor's in visiting him right now, so you'll have to wait a few minutes."

I thanked her and headed for the now-familiar visitor's lounge. "He was a little better" probably meant that he had managed to eat a whole cup of JELL-O at lunch. Big deal. But at least, I thought, that would be an improvement over yesterday's half cup, right? I could remember him running with his long, graceful stride, winning the quarter-mile at the New Jersey AAU state track meet his senior year of high school, so by comparison a cup of JELL-O was a pretty depressing victory.

I was in a foul mood as I walked into the lounge, but, conscious that I was dressed as a priest, I managed to give a sincere priest-smile to the two people who were chatting quietly on the sofa at the far end, near the big window that looked out on an expanse of gravel-covered roof. I didn't recognize them; they must have been visiting someone else. I slumped into a chair near the door to brood.

Despite my depressed mood and my anger, I found that being in a hospital still made me feel like praying, as it usually did. So, while I was waiting, I started to ask the Lord to help Bob to get stronger, to let him start measuring victories in bigger steps than cups of JELL-O. I asked Jesus to heal whatever was wrong with my brother. Then I started to think how the Lord also works through doctors and nurses and family and friends to do the actual work of curing people.

That's probably why Jesus put such emphasis on visiting the sick—he even said that our final reward or punishment would be based on it: "Come, you who are blessed by my Father, for I was sick and you visited me" (Matthew 25:36).

I glanced up at the big clock; I'd been sitting there for three long minutes waiting to visit my brother.

As far back as the Old Testament, the verb *episkeptomai*, "to visit"[4] had a deep religious meaning—mostly, I suppose, because the Israelites saw God as always "visiting" them. They knew God not as some theological abstraction, but as someone who was constantly intervening in the course of history to act on their behalf: to deliver them from Egypt, to knock down the walls of Jericho, or to restore the temple after the Babylonian Exile.

So when the Jewish scholars who were translating Old Testament Hebrew into Greek looked for a Greek word to express this idea of God's acting in their lives, they found that *episkeptomai* fit the bill perfectly: It meant both "to visit" and "to be concerned about." They used it, for instance, for the Lord's "looking on" Sarah so that she bore a son, Isaac (Genesis 21:1), and for the patriarch Joseph's deathbed prophecy that God would one day "look upon" his brothers and lead them out of Egypt (Genesis 50:24). The widowed Ruth decided to return to her native land because she heard that the long drought had ended because "the Lord had had consideration for [*episkeptomai*] his people" (Ruth 1:6).

The idea that God is constantly and deeply involved in the world carried over into the Christian era, so that in almost half the uses of "to visit" in the New Testament it is God who is doing the visiting. You can hear it in the cry of the amazed onlookers when Jesus raises the son of the widow of Naim: "Fear seized them all, and they glorified God, exclaiming, 'A great prophet has arisen in our midst,' and 'God has visited [*episkeptomai*] his people'" (Luke 7:16 NAB).

---

4. *Episkeptomai* (ep-ee-skep´-tom-ahee), from *epi*, "over," and *skop-/skep-*, "to see," means literally "to inspect," then "to go and see someone, to pay a visit." Saint Paul says to Barnabas, "Come, let us return and visit [*episkeptomai*] the believers in every city where we proclaimed the Lord and see how they are doing" (Acts 15:36).

I glanced up at the big electric clock. I'd been waiting for five minutes. I wondered if I should go and see if the doctor had left yet, but I decided to wait a little longer.

I kept reflecting about God's visiting. At Morning Prayer each day we sing the "Canticle of Zachary,"[5] which begins by praising our God who has "visited [*episkeptomai*] and brought redemption to his people" (Luke 1:68), and ends with "the tender mercy of our God by which the dawn from on high will visit [*episkeptomai*] us" (v. 78). In that first sentence, the two verbs "visited" and "redeemed" are a pair: They go together, and both mean the exact same thing. This "visiting God" is decidedly not dropping by for a quick hello, but has a clear purpose in mind: to redeem, to bring healing and salvation.

I smiled as I remembered what the nurse, Phyllis, had said back at the desk: "The doctor is in visiting him right now." I knew that Bob got billed every time a doctor made a "visit" to his bedside. Funny, one of the earliest uses of *episkeptomai* was for a doctor "visiting" a patient. Obviously the oncologist who was "visiting" Bob was not paying a social call, but had come as a healer with only one goal in mind: to cure Bob's lymphoma. Maybe that's why early believers started to use the word to refer to God's visiting us, because when the Almighty "visits" it's always to work some healing wonder in our lives.

I found myself praying again: "Lord, please visit Bob this afternoon, and stretch out your hand to touch him to comfort him and heal him. Help the doctor who is trying so hard to cure him, and visit the rest of us, too, with your strength." I had forgotten for the moment that God had been visiting Bob and the rest of us all along, and was certainly doing so right now, even as the doctor was visiting.

I glanced again at the clock. I'd now been sitting there ten minutes. That was long enough. I stood up and smiled good-by to the two people who were still sitting by the window. I wasn't looking forward

---

5. The so-called *Benedictus* (Luke 1:68–79) gets its name from its first line in Latin "Blessed [*Benedictus*] be the Lord, the God of Israel."

to seeing Bob all weak and wasting away, but I did want to go in and hold his hand and talk with him for awhile and just—well—visit.

Reflection

1. God's visits are life-giving and healing. Do your own interactions with others have the same results? Is there someone God may be expecting you to "visit" in a life-giving and healing way?

2. The verb *episkopeō* is used for a shepherd carefully watching his sheep (1 Peter 5:1–2) and gives us words for "overseer" in Greek (*episkopos*) and Latin (*episcopus*)—the early Church's words for "bishop." If there are people in your life over whom you have been given some charge (children, employees, students, an aging parent), ask yourself how your "overseeing" might also be a kind of blessed "visiting" for those in your care.

Sacred Scripture

Other texts that contain the verb *episkeptomai* offer plenty of food for meditation:

1. Ex 4:31, "the Lord had given heed to [*episkeptomai*] the Israelites."
2. Ps 106:4 (NAB), "Remember [*episkeptomai*] me, Lord, as you favor your people; come to me with your saving help."
3. Heb 2:6, "What are . . . mortals that you should care for [*episkeptomai*] them"?
4. James 1:27, "Religion that is pure and undefiled before God and the Father is this: to care for [*episkeptomai*] orphans and widows in their affliction. . . ."

Rule of Benedict

Care of the sick must rank above and before all else, so that they may truly be served as Christ, for he said: "I was sick and you visited me," and "What you did for one of these least brothers you did for me" (Chapter 36, "The Sick Brothers," vv. 1–3).

11. The God of Compassion

"WELL, AS FAR AS I'M CONCERNED, God killed my brother!"

Even as I was saying it I knew that what I was saying was untrue and sounded stupid. But what else are friends for if you can't tell them what you're feeling.

"No he didn't," my brother Benedictine replied calmly, gazing out at the view of New York City twenty miles away.

"Yes he did!" I retorted loudly.

"No he didn't," he answered in his same even tone. We repeated this a few more times until, seeing that he wasn't about to give in I gave up on the game.

We just stood there in silence, leaning on the stone wall that runs along the top of the cliff at Washington Rock, and watching tiny toy-sized jets landing at Newark Airport. Off to our left we could see in the far distance the pincushion of lower Manhattan crowded with the needles of dozens of shiny skyscrapers.

It had been only two weeks since my brother's death, the most painful experience of my life, and emotions were still raging and tumbling around inside me in confused tangles. I could see why people in ancient times thought that all strong emotions were located in the gut. That's certainly where I'd been feeling them.

In fact, the New Testament Greek word for affection or compassion is actually the plural noun *splanchna*,[6] meaning "the internal organs of the abdomen." We hear it in Mary's song of praise, the "Magnificat," in the phrase "because of the tender of mercy [the *splanchna*] of our God" (Luke 1:78).

For us Christians, this idea of a God who experiences "tender mercy," who suffers and who feels, is so familiar and so taken for

6. *Splanchna* (splangkh´-nah), bowels, affection, compassion. The verb *splanchnizomai* (splangkh-nid´-zom-ahee) means "to be moved with compassion, moved with

granted that we lose sight of its powerful implications. This is exactly what had happened to me after my brother's death. I had lost sight of those crucial Christian beliefs: that the risen Savior suffers when we suffer, that he weeps when we weep, and that he shares in all of our pains. I was furious at God for allowing my brother to die, leaving his wife, Judy, and four little children—which was why I'd just told my brother monk and hiking partner that God had killed my brother. It felt like a way of striking back. Although I'd been celebrating mass and praying with my community four times a day, for the past couple of weeks I had been so angry that I refused to speak to God.

Without another word we turned and starting walking the two miles back to the car along the road through the woods.

Jesus taught us that God is full of compassion. In the parable of the Unforgiving Servant, the servant who owed his master ten thousand talents of silver "fell down, did him homage, and said, 'Be patient with me, and I will pay you back in full.' Moved with compassion [*splanchnizomai*] the master of that servant let him go and forgave him the loan" (Matthew 18:26–27). In the story of the Prodigal Son, "While [the repentant son] was still a long way off, his father caught sight of him, and was filled with compassion [*splanchnizomai*]. He ran to his son, embraced him and kissed him" (Luke 15:20).

If Christ taught us about the compassion of our Father through parables, he showed his own compassion by performing miracles. Jesus was "moved with pity" to cleanse a leper in Mark 1:41 and to give sight to a group of blind men in Matthew 20:32–34. At the sight of the bereaved widow of Naim, who was about to bury her only son, "he was moved with pity [*splanchnizomai*] for her and said to her, 'Do not weep'" (Luke 7:13). The miracle of the loaves and fishes began with Jesus calling his disciples to him and saying, "I have compassion [*splanchnizomai*] for the crowd, because they have been with me now for three days and have nothing to eat" (Matthew 15:32). In all of these stories Jesus' compassion moved him to immediate and decisive action: immediately he cleansed the lepers; immediately he raised the young man from the dead; he responded immediately to the hunger of the crowd by feeding them with the miraculous loaves and fishes.

The gospels, then, show us both God the Father and God the Son being deeply moved at the sight of our human suffering. This idea that our God is overflowing with compassion and is moved in his deepest being by human suffering could have been a special comfort to me that afternoon as I was walking along that road through the woods. Unfortunately it would be a year or so after his death before I made the connection between that odd Greek word and how God must have been suffering terribly alongside Bob and us the whole time.

We paused at a clearing where another scenic overlook offered a view that extended more than twenty miles to the east to Brooklyn and Staten Island, and stretched far to the north to include most of Manhattan Island and to the south past Elizabeth and Linden. The view was entrancing mostly, I think, because of the wonderful sense of perspective it gave, letting us actually see how all the different cities and landmarks related to one another. The Verazzano Narrows Bridge, straight ahead, connected Brooklyn with Staten Island, and the rainbow-shaped Bayonne Bridge connected Staten Island with Bayonne, New Jersey. Closer to us stood the buildings of downtown Newark and the runways of Newark Airport, and between them and Manhattan was the empty space of the New Jersey Meadowlands. We turned away from the view and started walking again.

As my brother's death grows more distant in time, I've come to gain a lot of perspective on the experience and am able to see how so many of the events back then are interconnected. One thing that has been put into perspective is my anger at God. Looking back now I'm sure that the Lord understood and forgave my "silent treatment," and was patiently suffering with me and trying to help me get through that difficult time of grieving. In fact, I can now see that our relationship grew stronger because of my quarrel with God.

My hiking partner glanced at his watch and said, "Okay, vespers is in an hour and a half; we'll be okay if we just keep moving."

He was still calm and relaxed. I was still angry. And God? Well, I suppose the God of compassion was walking alongside me and feeling my pain—and perhaps getting ready to respond with a healing miracle.

Reflection

1. When or where have you experienced God's compassion and pity? Was it through another human being or in some other way?
2. The Good Samaritan of the parable is "moved with compassion" at the sight of the injured man and then acts on those feelings to take care of him (Luke 10:33–34). We become Christ-like not by feeling compassion for a needy neighbor, but by doing something to help that person. When are your feelings of compassion most likely to move you to help someone? When are such feelings more likely to remain just feelings?

Sacred Scripture

Some other passages where *splanchna*, "compassion" appears are Mark 6:34, 9:22; John 11:33; and Col 3:12.

Rule of Benedict

[The abbot] is to imitate the loving example of the Good Shepherd who left the ninety-nine sheep in the mountains and went in search of the one sheep that had strayed. So great was his compassion for its weakness that he mercifully placed it on his sacred shoulders and so carried it back to the flock (Chapter 27, "The Abbot's Concern for the Excommunicated," vv. 8–9).

12. Expanding My Heart

"THANKS FOR COMING, Father!"

"Happy to do it," I said, and asked "How're you doing? You okay?"

My fellow faculty member and I were standing facing his father's open casket in a crowded funeral parlor.

"Yeah. I'm fine, at least for now," he answered with a wry smile.

I stayed there with my arm around his shoulder, secretly wishing I could be somewhere else. Anywhere else. My friend had no idea how hard it was for me to be there. It was still the summer of Bob's death, and everything brought back memories of his wake just six weeks before: the hushed murmur of voices, the cloying fragrance of the big floral arrangements, the displays of old photos, a homemade card with a childish crayon drawing and "I love you Grandpa" printed in big block letters.

My eyes started to fill with tears, so I hurriedly blurted out, "Well, listen, I guess I better be going. I promise I'll be praying for you tomorrow morning, but I won't be able to make it to the funeral mass."

As I gave my colleague a parting hug, I had a rather un-priestly thought: "Thank God I can't be at the funeral!" This quick visit to the wake had been hard enough. For the past six weeks since Bob died I'd been in a wilderness of pain worse than anything I had ever experienced before. My heart was numb with sorrow. Until this evening I had successfully avoided attending wakes because they would have been too painful, reopening the fresh wound of Bob's death.

It would take me a few more weeks before the tide of suffering receded enough that I could really start caring once again about other people's problems, especially their grief. Quite understandably, I felt that I had more than enough of my own sadness and sorrow to deal with without worrying about the sadness and sorrow of others.

There is a biblical image that describes the way I felt that evening: My heart was "too full." It is based on the Greek verb *chōreō*, "to contain, to make room."[7] Jesus used this word when he saw that the minds and hearts of the Pharisees were completely filled with concern for the precise observance of legal minutiae and the detailed dictates of Jewish ritual prescriptions; he complained to them, "there is no place [*chōreō*] in you for my word" (John 8:37 NRSV). Their hundreds of ritual prescriptions and regulations had left no room in the Pharisees' hearts for God to do anything new with them.

Once when some Corinthians were harboring bad feelings toward Paul, he wrote asking them to not let jealousy or pettiness crowd out Christian love; he pleaded "Make room [*chōreō*] for us. . . ." (2 Corinthians 7:2). The *New Jerusalem Bible* translates this request very beautifully as "Keep a place for us in your hearts."

In the same letter Paul combines *chōreō* "to have room" and the adjective *stenos,* "narrow," into a single ominous word, *stenochōreō*.[8] He uses it to describe certain Christians who were acting out of jealousy and envy; he accuses them of "narrowing their hearts." A free translation of the passage might be: "We have spoken frankly to you, Corinthians, and we have opened wide our hearts. We have not narrowed our hearts to you, but you have narrowed [*stenochōreō*] yours" (2 Corinthians 6:11–12). Here the problem is not that they have no room in their hearts, but worse, that their hearts are actually getting smaller!

I kept working my way toward the exit at the back of the crowded funeral parlor, offering brief "hellos" and handshakes as I went. I moved as quickly as I decently could, and managed not to break into a run in my haste to escape.

---

7. *Chōreō* (kho-reh´-o), "to contain, to make room." John tells us that if he were to record all of Jesus' deeds, "the whole world could not contain [*chōreō*] the books it would take" (John 21:25).

8. The verb *stenochōreō* (sten-okh-o-reh´-o) means literally "to make narrow," and figuratively "to be constrained" (see 2 Corinthians 4:8).

My heart was definitely full of grief that evening, with little room left for other concerns. In fact I suppose you could say that the pain had even made my heart grow narrower.

But it turned out that this was only a necessary step in a process, as when a wound tightens and constricts as it starts to heal. The next months were a time of slow, imperceptible healing. In the end I found that somehow my heart had actually become wider, not narrower; it had been painfully, permanently stretched. As a result, when I attend a wake or a funeral today, it is as someone whose heart has been expanded by grief, someone who has experienced what the mourners are experiencing. Countless times since that awful night I've been able to help people who were facing the monster of grief. I've quietly stood beside them and whispered "I've been there, too." I've reassured them that it was okay if their heart was completely full of sorrow at the time, and that I knew what it was like when pain made your heart shrink so that you didn't care about anyone else's problems. More than once I've whispered to someone, "Yup, I know what that's like. Believe me!"

But back on that evening as I hurried toward the exit of the funeral home, my grieving heart was still too full, too narrow. But at least I'd shown up at the wake—maybe my heart was already starting to stretch a little.

For Reflection

1. Paul accuses some of his Corinthian readers of "narrowing their hearts" (2 Cor 7:2). Have you ever felt your heart "narrowing" toward someone? Were you aware of what was causing this? Were you able to overcome the impulse? If so, how?

2. Has your own experience of suffering made you more aware of the suffering of others, and perhaps more able to be of help to them?

3. Reflect on how Paul's plea for an "open heart" might apply to broader areas such as ecumenism, the conservative-liberal debate, or the issues of race and immigration.

Sacred Scripture

The literal meaning of *chōreō*, "to contain, to make room for" can add
to a deeper understanding of each of the following two passages:

1. "But he said to them, 'Not everyone can accept [*chōreō* = make
   room for] this teaching, but only those to whom it is given"
   (Matt 19:11).

2. "The Lord is not slow about his promise, as some think of slow-
   ness, but is patient with you, not wanting any to perish, but all to
   come to [*chōreō* = have room for] repentance" (2 Pet 3:9).

Rule of Benedict

But as we progress in this way of life and in faith, we shall run on the
path of God's commandments, our hearts expanded with the inexpress-
ible delight of love (Prologue, v. 49, author's trans.).

CHAPTER FOUR

My Turn with the Monster

Cancer

When I heard that my brother Richard, ten years older than I, had been diagnosed with prostate cancer in 2000, I was of course worried for him, and couldn't help thinking of Bob's cancer and death. But deep inside I was also afraid for myself, because his illness put me into the "high risk" category for the same disease. So I dutifully went to the doctor to begin keeping a wary eye on the PSA level in my blood. The first couple of biopsies were negative. Then what I'd been fearing for almost three years finally happened: a biopsy came back positive. I had cancer.

The cancer had been detected early, was not an especially virulent type, and was easily treatable. I was fortunate to be able to have the new robotic surgery to remove my prostate, an operation which required just an overnight stay in the hospital. It was successful and within a few weeks the discomfort and the worst side effects of the surgery were past. My life returned to normal, and I've been cancer-free ever since.

Except for the initial shock, this did not turn out to be a particularly terrible ordeal; in fact, it was all over so quickly and with such minimal pain that I do not consider myself to have earned the proud title of "cancer survivor." Yet I certainly discovered a lot about myself during this period. Thanks to what I had learned from dealing with the demise and resurrection of Saint Benedict's Prep and with Bob's death, I was able even as I was going through this experience to see it as a mysterious opportunity from God. All along, starting with the diagnosis and through the process of healing after the operation, I spent a lot of time praying and thinking about what the Lord might be trying to teach me. The following meditations offer some of my reflections and reactions during that time.

13. Calling for Help

I WALKED ACROSS THE PARKING LOT toward my car studying the little white business card in my hand. Filled in neatly with a blue ballpoint pen were the date and time of my follow-up visit with the urologist: I was scheduled to come back in ten days to find out the results of today's biopsy, my third. A couple of minutes before, the doctor had told me very matter-of-factly, "It usually takes about a week to get the results back from the lab. So let's make an appointment so I can see you in about eight or ten days." He, like everyone else in the office, had seemed in no big rush to find out whether or not I had prostate cancer. Ten days, I thought to myself as I unlocked the car door, is an awful long time to wait for news that can change or even end your life! And this time for some reason I was worried about the results. But there was nothing to do now but wait. And of course pray for God's help—which is what I was doing as I unlocked the car door and got into the driver's seat.

Asking God for help comes naturally to most believers. It's something most of us do all the time without giving it much thought. Every day we monks begin both Midday and Evening Prayer with the opening verse of Psalm 70: "O God, come to my assistance, O Lord, make haste to help me" (Psalm 70:1). Christians call for God's help in their hymns such as "O God, our help in ages past," and in dozens of formal orations, "Almighty Lord, we come before you seeking your divine aid. . . ." In fact the word "help" is so common in our prayer and worship that we hardly even notice that we're saying it.

But, as I sat there praying that afternoon, I was intensely aware of what I was asking for: Help!

It's actually quite an interesting word in the Bible. In the Septuagint (Greek) translation of the Old Testament the verb *boētheō*, "to help"[1] is a synonym for "save" or "redeem," as for example in Psalm 37,

---

1. *Boētheō* (bo-ay-theh´-o), "to help, assist;" from *boē*, "a shout for aid," and *theō*, "to run."

"the Lord helps them and rescues them" (Psalm 37:40) where "helps" is simply another word for "rescues." In Psalm 44, "to help" means "to redeem" when the psalmist prays, "Rise up, help us! Redeem us as your love demands" (Psalm 44:27).

In the gospels, the verb is used by troubled people who are approaching Jesus. A Canaanite mother whose daughter is being tormented by a demon "came and did [Jesus] homage, saying, Lord, help [boētheō] me" (Matthew 15:25). A father whose son is possessed by a mute spirit pleads: "But if you can do anything, have compassion on us and help [boētheō] us" (Mark 9:22).[2]

As I started the engine, I thought of how the author of Hebrews encourages his readers to "confidently approach the throne of grace to receive mercy and to find grace for timely help" (Hebrews 4:16). Well, I said to myself, I guess that's exactly what I'm looking for, "timely help."

Then I remembered a striking image from the Acts of the Apostles that fit my situation perfectly. The ship carrying Saint Paul to Rome for

trial was suddenly overtaken by a terrible storm that lasted for days. As towering waves began to smash down onto the vessel, threatening to break it apart, the desperate sailors "used cables to undergird the ship" (Acts 27:17). The Greek word for these cables that were holding the ship together is boētheiais, literally, "helps."[3]

I pictured myself about to enter some very stormy seas if the biopsy came back positive for cancer. I started to ask the Lord to wrap me round with some of those "helps," and pull them good and tight around me to keep me from breaking apart under the giant waves.

I put the car in reverse and backed carefully out of the narrow parking space, kind of like a captain slowly guiding his ship away from

2. When Jesus assures him that everything is possible to one who has faith, the boy's father cries out, "I do believe, help [boētheō] my unbelief" (Mark 9: 24).

3. The plural form of the noun boētheia (bo-ay´-thi-ah), "help, assistance."

a dock. The image of a storm-tossed vessel being held together by heavy ropes might not be the first one to come to mind for most modern Christians, but it worked for me that afternoon.

In fact, it's still my favorite way of picturing God's timely help.

Reflection

1. Read Acts 27:9–44, Luke's vivid account of the storm at sea. Take your time. Imagine yourself as a frightened passenger below decks listening to the howling of the tempest and the ominous creaking of the ship's timbers. Watch the leaks appear in the sides of the boat. Climb up onto the deck and feel it pitching and heaving; hear the wind howl as it hurls mountainous waves onto the ship for hours on end; watch as the panicking sailors wrap "helps" around the ship's midsection in a desperate attempt to keep it from breaking apart. How do you feel when you see those cables?

   Now think of a crisis in your life which felt like that furious storm. Did you ask for God's help right away? Was the Lord a "help" to you at the time by "holding you together?" If so, what specific form did those "helps" take: a person? an insight? an event? Were you aware of the divine help at the time?

2. The Letter to the Hebrews tells us that Jesus' experience of suffering made him able to help others: "Because he himself was tested through what he suffered, he is able to help [*boētheō*] those who are being tested" (Heb 2:18). Reflect on how your sufferings have made you more able to help a brother or sister in need.

Sacred Scripture

The verb *boētheō*, "to help" appears in Isa 41:10; Acts 16:9, 21:28; Heb 2:18; and the noun form "helper" in Heb 13:6.

Rule of Benedict

First of all, every time you begin a good work, you must pray to him most earnestly to bring it to perfection (Prologue, v. 4).

14. Lying Down in Green Pastures

I FELT VAGUELY UNEASY as I sat in the urologist's waiting room with five other people. For the past few years, ever since my brother's bout with prostate cancer had put me in the high-risk category, I'd been dutifully visiting this office for regular biopsies. The first two had both come back negative, but I had a suspicion that the results this time might be different. My PSA levels had been looking strange on the last couple of blood tests. I had no real reason to worry, I told myself as I picked up an old *Newsweek* and started thumbing through it. Then when I reminded myself that both my mom and my brother Bob had died of cancer, I tossed the magazine back on the table right away—my mind was elsewhere.

As people who know me well can tell you, I'm the type of person who tends to worry about things just as a matter of course. So I should have been a bundle of nerves sitting there; but in fact I was fairly relaxed. This was probably because I had been consciously keeping in front of me all day an image from my morning meditation: a sheep lying down confidently in a green pasture under the shepherd's watchful eye.

"Father Holtz!" The emotionless voice of a white-coated medical assistant startled me back to the present. I tried to read his poker face as he held the door for me. Did I see something unusually solemn in his expression or was I just imagining it? I stepped nervously into the long, brightly lit corridor lined with doors along the right side. He showed me through the first door on the right. "The doctor will be with you in a moment," he said, as he closed the door, leaving me alone in the formal office.

I sat down in a big brown leather armchair and glanced around the bright, friendly room, its wood paneling set off by a couple of cheerful landscape paintings and some very impressive-looking diplomas. But I deliberately turned my mind back to the comforting image of the green pasture and the trusting sheep lying on the grass; I was still there when the door opened and the doctor walked in.

I stood up and shook his hand, then sank down again in the comfortable leather chair. I peered at him across the wide expanse of the polished desktop trying to read the expression on his kind face. Sensing my anxiety he got right to the point: "Well, Father," he began in his quiet, gentle voice as he glanced at the open folder in front of him, "we got the biopsy report back. The results were positive; I'm afraid they found some cancer."

"They found some cancer." Thousands of cancer patients have told of the terror they felt when they first heard that horrifying diagnosis, and of how their world was shattered into pieces. Knowing that this was the normal reaction, I was immediately surprised at how peaceful I was. Maybe those decades of meditating and of trying to trust God more were bearing some fruit. In any case I heard the doctor's dire news while seated on the green grass of Psalm 23 and sustained by an overwhelming sense of being taken care of by the Lord. Of course my stomach tightened and I found it hard to focus on all the details of the kind of cancer it was and the doctor's recitation of the pros and cons of various treatment options. But the most striking recollection I would have of that afternoon would be the image of that green pasture of the "Good Shepherd" psalm. I was lying down on the grass and trusting in the shepherd to keep me safe.

This picture had come to me earlier that morning as I was reflecting on Matthew's account of the miracle of the loaves and fishes (Matthew 15:32–38). I was struck by verse 35: "Then ordering the crowd to sit down on the ground. . . ."[4] I knew that "sit down" was a translation of one of my favorite Greek words, *anapiptō*.[5] What had

---

4. In Matthew's earlier version of the miracle, this verse reads "sit down on the green grass" (Matthew 14:19).

5. The verb *anapiptō* (ah-nah-pip′-to), "to lean backwards, recline, dine," comes from *ana*, "back, backwards," + *piptō*, "fall," and means literally "to fall backwards."

first interested me about the word was that it means literally "to fall backwards, to lean back." For instance, when Jesus reveals at the last supper that someone is about to betray him, "the disciple whom Jesus loved" leaned back [*anapiptō*] against his chest and asked him, "Master, who is it?" (John 13:25).

Usually, however, the verb is not used in this literal way but in the sense of "to lean back to dine." For solemn meals, Jews in New Testament times followed the Roman custom of lying on mats or low couches around the outside edge of a low U-shaped table. The diners would lean on their left elbow and use their right hand for eating. This was the scene, for instance, when Our Lord accepted a Pharisee's invitation to dinner: "Jesus entered and reclined at table [*anapiptō*] to eat" (Luke 11:37). Since this was a banquet, Jesus and the others would literally have "reclined" as they ate.[6] Early on, however, the word expanded from its narrow meaning of "to recline at a banquet" to become the general word for "to sit down to eat."

This is the word I had come upon at the beginning of the story of the loaves and fishes early in the morning on the day I was going to find out the biopsy results: ". . . he ordered the crowds to sit down on the grass." Ever since discovering the background of this word, I've loved the image of thousands of hungry people in that deserted spot not simply sitting down to eat, but obediently "leaning over backwards" in trust at Jesus' invitation.

That morning I had wondered what I would have done if I'd been in that crowd when Jesus invited them to sit down to eat. Being a doer by nature, and someone who wants to solve his own problems, I had trouble imagining myself leaning back passively and letting him supply me with food. I would have preferred instead to find some way of getting it for myself. But as I continued my morning meditation, I eventually managed to picture myself "reclining" on the grass. And then, remembering

---

6. This posture explains how a woman could "stand behind Jesus at his feet" during a banquet and begin to wash his feet with her tears (Luke 7:38).

the literal meaning of the word, I had closed my eyes and let myself "fall backwards," knowing that he would catch me, and that he would give me whatever strength I might need to get through this or any ordeal.

"So, give it some thought, Father." The doctor's voice pulled me back into the world of biopsy results and treatment options. "It's not an emergency, but I wouldn't wait too long, either. It needs to be taken care of."

I agreed to give him a call in a couple of days with my decision about what I wanted to do about treatment. Then we stood up and shook hands. As I headed for the door I took a quick glance back at the big brown armchair. True, for the past twenty minutes I hadn't really been sitting on green grass, but that chair had actually done just as well.

Reflection

Think of a particularly difficult time in your life when the Lord was inviting you into a wilderness and asking you to lie down trustingly on the grass. What was the most difficult part of the experience? Did you manage to hand the problem over to God or did you hang on and work it out on your own?

Sacred Scripture

The verb *anapiptō* in the sense of "recline at table" appears in Tob 2:1; Luke 17:7, 22:14.

Rule of Benedict

Now, therefore, after ascending all these steps of humility, the monk will quickly arrive at that perfect love of God which casts out fear (Chapter 7 "Humility," v. 67).

15. You of Little Faith

I WAS LYING ON A NARROW HOSPITAL GURNEY staring up at the bright fluorescent lights in the ceiling of the pre-op room where I and several other patients were waiting to be wheeled into surgery. I turned my head and sneaked a quick, nervous glance down at the blue plastic anesthesia shunt sticking out of my left forearm and wondered if the anesthetist would come and introduce himself as I'd been promised. So far I'd managed to be fairly calm; I hoped I could stay that way until the whole operation was over. I tried not to think about it. . . . I started to mechanically rattle off a few Hail Marys. This had a soothing effect, as it always does at stressful moments, but then I started to get more personal, more specific: "Lord, please help the doctors and nurses during the operation, and help me too. Watch over all the other people in this room and keep them safe. Let each of us have a successful surgery and a good recovery. Help me to trust in your goodness no matter what happens."

"No matter what happens." Saying that made my stomach tighten, but it was important for me to add it. I knew from experience that, as long as everything was going smoothly, my faith would be strong, but if things started to go wrong, my faith might not stand up too well.

But at least I was in good company, I thought. Even the apostles used to fold under pressure. Once when the boat they were in was being swamped by waves during a sudden squall, they woke Jesus up and shouted, Lord, save us! We're going to drown! He scolded them, "Why are you terrified, you of little faith?" (Matthew 8:25–26).

I lay there comforted as much by the idea of the apostles' weakness as by Jesus' presence. I kept thinking about that scene. "O you of little faith" is actually a single word in Greek, *oligopistos*.[7] It describes

---

7. The adjective *oligopistos* (ol-ig-op´-is-tos) comes from *oligos* (ol-ee´-gos), "few, little" and *pistis* (pis´-tis), "faith, trust."

someone who has faith but just not enough of it at certain stressful times. Hmmm. Just like me, I guess—and the apostles.

Actually Saint Peter himself struggled with the problem, too. Once when the disciples were out in their boat, they were caught in a fierce storm—it seems like they were always getting caught in fierce storms—and were being tossed about by the wind and the waves. Suddenly Jesus appeared, walking toward them on the water. They figured it must be a ghost until he spoke and invited Peter to walk toward him on the water. So Peter jumped out of the boat and started walking. But when he saw how strong the wind was, Peter got scared and started to sink and shouted, "Lord, save me!" Jesus stretched out his hand and grabbed him, and said, "You of little faith [*oligopistos*]! Why did you doubt?'" (Matthew 14: 31).

Following Jesus as he wandered around preaching and healing, Peter had been busy taking care of a lot of practical details and trying to absorb all the lessons that Jesus was giving the apostles. Although he kept saying that he believed that Jesus was the Messiah, Peter's faith in him hadn't really been tested at all.

A woman in green scrubs and a puffy cloth hat covering her hair came in and asked how I was doing. "I'm good, thanks," I told her. She checked my ID-wristband and patted my arm. "It'll be just a few minutes now, okay?" "Yes. Fine," I replied, "I'll be here."

I kept thinking about Peter walking on the waves. He started listening to the raging wind and watching the angry waves and realized that things were getting way beyond his control. Then the poor guy lost his nerve completely. Boy, do I know how that feels!

Interesting, though. Each and every time that the apostles were panicking and were accused of being "of little faith," Jesus had been right there with them the whole time, either standing nearby or even sitting with them in the boat. All the stories always end the same way: The apostles realize they're not alone and that they don't have to depend just on their own puny powers, because Christ, the divine Son of God almighty, is right there. Once they open their eyes to the fact that Jesus is there beside them, their "little faith" suddenly becomes more than enough to carry them through.

Two people came in and wheeled out the old woman on the gurney next to mine. I guessed that I would probably be next. I tried not to think about it.

My own life, I thought, is a mixture of faith and doubt, just like the apostles'. One minute things are going along smoothly and I'm full of calm confidence. Then a sudden squall starts to swamp my boat and I do what Peter did—I panic. I forget that Jesus is right there with me. But then, above the howling wind and the roaring waves, I hear a gentle, familiar voice call with infinite patience and tenderness: "You of little faith!"

Sometimes he comes in a word or a warm smile from a friend. At other times he comes in a sudden insight from something I have heard or read. Or perhaps in a deep feeling of peace while I'm praying. It's as if in the midst of the storm Jesus has just reached down and taken my hand firmly in his own.

I felt a strong hand grasping mine, and, startled, I opened my eyes to look up at a man in a green scrub suit who was introducing himself as the anesthetist. His calm, confident voice was reassuring; so was his firm grip as he held onto my hand for a moment and asked me, "So, Albert, are you ready?"

I half expected him to add, "O you of little faith!"

Reflection

1. Has Jesus ever revealed himself sitting next to you in the midst of danger or in a time of trouble? If so, how did he show his presence? Was it through some particular "coincidence" or event? Through a word of encouragement from a friend? Or perhaps in some unexpected help from a stranger?

2. Read the story of the apostles caught in the storm on the Sea of Galilee in Matt 8:23–26. Take your time; try to put yourself in

the apostles' place in the boat. Share their feelings, especially the change from terror to relief. Ask the Lord to increase and strengthen your faith.

Sacred Scripture

Oligopistos appears also in Matt 6:30, 16:5–12, and 17:20.

Rule of Benedict

What is not possible to us by nature, let us ask the Lord to supply by the help of his grace (Prologue, v. 41).

16. A New Sense of Time

MY NIECE, NANCY, who happens also to be my goddaughter, was sitting at her kitchen table with a mug of morning coffee and sharing with me some of what she had learned from her battle with breast cancer. My own recent bout of cancer had given the two of us a new closeness, which we were thoroughly enjoying that morning. She was describing the day when she'd found out that she had breast cancer.

"We all know we're going to die sooner or later but we all assume that it'll be later," she said. "When I was diagnosed with cancer I suddenly realized that it might actually be sooner, like now—this year, maybe even next month."

She went on: "Once during those first weeks when I was still in shock I remember I was planting flowers in our new garden, just enjoying the sunshine, and glancing at Paul [her husband] mowing the lawn. And suddenly I got this intense appreciation of the moment. After the cancer diagnosis I now I had this sharp, fierce appreciation of every aspect of every minute I was alive."

With a voice that reflected a mixture of gratitude and conviction, she added, "I still have it, and now I'll stop and notice—really notice—things I wouldn't have even seen before. Like the clouds, say, or the way a tree branch is moving, or the color of someone's lipstick."

Just then the sound of excited chirping started outside and we both turned to look out the window to watch the loud commotion at the bird feeder hanging on a tree in the backyard. When I turned back to look at Nancy, I noticed how healthy and happy she looked now. The awful weakness and nausea from chemotherapy seemed like ages ago, and her hair had long since grown back. She'd been in remission for four years at that point.

I started to think about her new appreciation of time. Time was no longer something she took for granted by letting the minutes slip through her fingers unnoticed.

My niece, I thought to myself, had come to the same conclusion as the New Testament writers: Every moment we're alive is a special time. They had an easier way to express this idea than we do, however, since they had two different words for time.

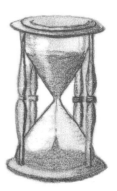

First there was *chronos*,[8] which referred to time as something measurable and divisible into quantities; you counted it off in months, minutes, and milliseconds. In the Parable of the Talents, a master goes off on a journey and returns "after a long time [*chronos*]" (Matthew 25:19). We are all well acquainted with this sort of time. We save time by taking a short-cut to avoid traffic, we waste time doing things that serve no purpose, we even kill time in the airport waiting for our flight.

The second Greek word for time was *kairos*.[9] Unlike *chronos* (time as measured off in minutes and hours), *kairos* referred to time as having significance: time as an event, an occasion, or an opportunity. This is the kind of time we mean when we say "It's high time" or "I had a great time."

Kairos actually had a variety of meanings in the Bible. It is often translated "season"—that is, a time for some specific purpose, such as harvesting, as in the familiar passage in Ecclesiastes 3:1–8, "A time [*kairos*] to be born and a time [*kairos*] to die.[10] It also had the sense of "a suitable time, an opportunity": the faithful servant in charge of the household will "distribute food to them at the due time [at the *kairos*]" (Matthew 24:45).

---

8. *Chronos* (khron´-os), "clock time, time as measurable, divisible into units"; it is found in such English words as "chronological" and "chronometer."

9. *Kairos* (kahee-ros´), "time as an event, an occasion; season."

10. When Jesus walked up to a fig tree, he found no fruit on it because "it was not the season [*kairos*] for figs" (Mark 11:13).

Now she was warming up to her topic. I could hear it in her voice: "Another thing I noticed was that, all of a sudden, I started to see that good intentions don't mean a thing—they don't count. At your eulogy nobody talks about what you planned to do or say. They only point out what you actually did and said. Because that's what counts, you know? So I started to realize that anything I want to do I have to do now because I might not have tomorrow. Looking at it this way has made my whole life better and more meaningful; it reminds me not to put off compliments to friends or loving words to my family—or having fun."

The sacred writers used *kairos* to express exactly that feeling of urgency, to point out an opportunity not to be missed. "Behold, now is the acceptable time [the acceptable *kairos*], now is the day of salvation" (2 Corinthians 6:2).

Listening to Nancy was reminding me to treat my own life as a *kairos*. After all, nothing says that my next blood test won't show a recurrence of cancer, so I may as well start to enjoy the beauty and goodness of the people and things around me right now, just the way she does.

We were both watching a bright red cardinal that was now alone at the bird feeder. He took two nervous pecks at the seeds and then darted away. I smelled the aroma drifting from the coffee pot, and noticed the way the early morning sun was using a thin curtain to paint patterns on the windowsill.

"Isn't life good?" I thought half aloud. Nancy had heard the comment, though. She looked right into my eyes and smiled.

"Yup," she said with absolute conviction, "It certainly is!"

Reflection

1. Think of an event, perhaps even an unpleasant one, that gave you a better appreciation of the things and people around you.

2. Think of some good intention you've had for awhile but have not acted on. Maybe now is a *kairos*, the "acceptable time" for you to finally put it into practice?

Sacred Scripture

Chronos is found in Matt 2:7; John 5:6; and Acts 18:20.

Kairos is found in Mark 12:12; Acts 14:17; and 1 Cor 4:5.

Rule of Benedict

Let us open our eyes to the light that comes from God, and our ears to the voice from heaven that every day calls out this charge: "If you hear his voice today, do not harden your hearts," and again: "You that have ears to hear, listen to what the Spirit says to the churches." And what does he say? "Come and listen to me, sons; I will teach you the fear of the Lord. Run while you have the light of life, that the darkness of death may not overtake you" (Prologue, vv. 9–13).

CHAPTER FIVE

WELCOMING MYSTERY
Our Community Grows Smaller

When I joined the monastery in 1962, monasticism—like most other religious institutions—was riding the crest of a great wave of new members. This was the era when American religious orders of both men and women launched ambitious building projects to house the scores of postulants and novices who were pouring in, and to provide more room for their thriving schools and colleges. After a consulting firm projected that our community in Newark would soon double in size, we hired an architect to make preliminary sketches of a spacious new monastery to accommodate all those new monks—a new monastery that was never to be built. Like all other American religious, we just assumed that things would keep getting bigger and better indefinitely, so no one was expecting what happened next.

The 1960s was the era of John F. Kennedy and the Peace Corps, the new thinking of the Second Vatican Council, the Civil Rights and Women's Rights movements, and Vietnam War protests. The world was changing rapidly, and religious life along with it. Within the space of a few years, not only did the flood of new vocations dry up, but vast numbers of religious and priests both old and young began leaving their religious calling in favor of the lay state. Our monastery suffered the same dramatic losses as other institutions.

The decline in numbers started in the 1960s, and in the intervening years, despite our efforts, there have been precious few people joining our monastery—nowhere near enough to replace the members who have died or have left. The projections for the future are sobering. How my brothers and I view the present and the future of our shrinking community and how we choose to respond will certainly reveal a lot about our faith in God.

The sections that follow offer some reflections on the way we are trying to respond to and grow from the challenge.

17. The Other Side of God

WE WERE AT SUPPER IN THE REFECTORY, fifteen monks at long wooden tables. Five tall windows lining the wall to my left gave a view of the cloister garden. There was always something to see in the garden at any time of year—especially the bright yellow flowers in summer, and the muted tones of chrysanthemums in the fall. My favorite is winter when the grass and shrubs are hidden under the graceful curves of deep, drifting snow.

The brother who was table-reader for the week had just finished reading a chapter from the Rule of Benedict, and was pausing before continuing the latest table-reading book, a biography of Abbot Boniface Wimmer, who founded the first Benedictine abbey in America. Across the room two monks were sitting at a table that was set for eight. I said to myself that when I first came here in 1969, there had been no empty places; there had been well over thirty of us then. But our community had been getting smaller for years now, a combination of older members passing away and no new ones coming to take their places.

This was the down side of each Benedictine abbey being totally independent—we monks don't get switched around to different monasteries, but stay in the same one our whole life.

A quick movement in the corner of my eye drew my attention back to the garden. The blustery winds of hurricane Floyd were causing a wild scene, whipping the shrubs back and forth and bending the taller flowers flat to the ground. Although the sky was ominously dark, it hadn't started raining yet. But the predicted gusts of up to sixty miles an hour had started an hour ago during mass.

Over near the window I noticed more empty places at tables, eloquent reminders that the God who had once given us comfortable prosperity was now leading us through some trying times. That evening there seemed to be no sign of the gracious God who had smiled down on us in the boom years of the early 1960s. Or maybe, it occurred to me, we were just seeing another side of God, one that we were not so familiar with.

The wind was now whistling in violent bursts, rippling the screens outside the tightly closed windows. "The sound as of a strong, driving wind," I said to myself, echoing Luke's description of the coming of the Holy Spirit at Pentecost.

I started to think of the ways in which that story points out the other, unsettling side of God. Those tongues of fire that appear above each apostle's head (Acts 2:3) are a good example. Fire is never used in Scripture as a symbol of peace or contentment; it is a means of purifying or even destroying. In Isaiah "tongues of fire" is an image of destructive power: "As the tongue of fire devours the stubble. . . ." (Isaiah 5:24). The fire at Pentecost warns us, the way the Letter to the Hebrews does, that "Our God is a consuming fire" (Hebrews 12:29).[1] For those of us who have ever felt the searing, purifying fire of God's sudden and unwelcome intervention in our lives, those tongues of divine fire are hardly a soothing image!

A particularly loud gust of wind made several heads look up from their supper and glance uneasily toward the window. I smiled as I thought that this is what it must have sounded like at Pentecost: "They were all in one place together. And suddenly there came from the sky a noise like a strong, driving wind, and it filled the entire house where they were" (Acts 2:1–2). That wind is a clear warning that what is about to happen in that room is not going to be soothing or calming—in fact it will be anything but. The Greek says literally "And there came suddenly out of heaven a sound as of a rushing, violent wind" (Acts 2:2). Luke uses the word "violent," *biaios*,[2] to

---

1. John the Baptist uses the image of fire three times within a few verses: "Therefore every tree that does not produce good fruit will be cut down and thrown into the fire. . . . He will baptize you with the Holy Spirit and fire. . . . the chaff he will burn with unquenchable fire" (Luke 3:9, 16–17).

2. The noun *bia* (bee´-ah) means "violence, physical force," as in "the *violence* of the mob" in Acts 21:35. The adjective describing the wind in the Pentecost story is *biaios* (bee´-ah-yos), "violent."

evoke a sense of energy and power unleashed. He uses it later in Acts when a captain deliberately runs his ship aground during a fierce storm and the stern is shattered to pieces "under the violence [*bia*] of the waves" (Acts 27:41). This kind of destructive force describes the sort of wind that Luke is talking 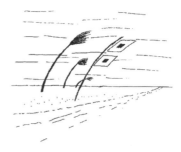 about at Pentecost: The Holy Spirit is not a gentle breeze, but a gale force wind.

Hurricane Floyd continued to howl in the background as the reader continued the story of Archabbot Boniface Wimmer. It seems that there was dissention among the monks of his monastery, Saint Vincent Archabbey in Latrobe, Pennsylvania. Two monks had written to Rome to complain about the conditions in their monastery. As a result, an official letter had been sent to Wimmer from Rome:

> The letter struck Wimmer like a lightning bolt. The seventy-three-year-old abbot reeled back from the blow in shock and dismay and wrote to Abbot Innocent Wolf of Kansas: "Father Maurice and Father Prior have brought accusations against me at the Vatican to the Pope. They have made charges for a hearing. The affair will probably end with my resignation."[3]

Sometimes, I thought to myself as I listened to the reading, the wind of the Spirit roars into the life of a community or into an individual's life to upset our cozy existence and uproot our favorite prejudices and assumptions about God and about everything else. Our community is certainly seeing this other side of God, and we have to keep praying that we will stay open to the work of the Spirit that troubles the waters, since that's the same Spirit that gives new life and renews the face of the earth.

3. Jerome Oetgen, *An American Abbot: Boniface Wimmer, O.S.B., 1809–1887* (rev. ed.; Washington, DC: Catholic University of America Press, 1997), 369.

As the storm continued outside, the reader continued the story of the struggles of the beleaguered archabbot and his community in 1871, and I, noticing the empty chairs again, wondered what the Spirit might be up to in our community in 1999.

Reflection

1. "In the beginning, when God created the heavens and the earth, the earth was a formless wasteland, and darkness covered the abyss, while a mighty wind swept over the waters" (Gen 1:1–2 NAB). Early Christian writers were fond of interpreting the wind troubling the waters as the Spirit, God's creative energy at work. When has God's troubling, creative wind blown in your life? How did you react?

2. Do you agree that the present upheavals in the church are opportunities for new growth? Have you experienced this in your own dealings with the church?

Sacred Scripture

Both the noun "violence" [*bia*] and the adjective "violent" [*biaios*] are found Matt 11:12; the related verb "to apply force" is in Luke 16:16.

Wisdom of the Desert

Abba Sisoes the Theban said to his disciple: "Tell me what you see in me and in turn I will tell you what I see in you." His disciple said to him: "You are good in soul, but a little harsh." The old man said to him: "You are good but your soul is not tough."[4]

---

4. Gregory Mayers, *Listen to the Desert: Secrets of Spiritual Maturity from the Desert Fathers and Mothers* (Liguori, Missouri: Triumph Books, 1996), 77.

18. Learning How to Worry

I WAS APPOINTED THE ABBEY'S DIRECTOR OF VOCATIONS, charged with both welcoming inquirers interested in joining the monastery and publicizing Newark Abbey so that people would know that there is a Benedictine abbey a few miles from New York City. We advertised, we developed a website, and we ran Holy Week retreats. As the years went on, however, we got fewer and fewer inquiries—it was clear that despite our best efforts at recruitment, the community was still getting smaller and smaller.

I used to worry a lot, not only about the lack of new candidates but also about my jobs in school: Would I get all the students entered onto the correct rosters? Would I have the schedules printed out in time? Would I be able to get my own classes prepared? Then, some years ago I was given a sabbatical year during which I traveled around Europe and South America staying in monasteries and then worked for a month in a parish in Bolivia. On the first day of this eleven-month journey, the moment I landed in Paris I felt myself begin to relax. No deadlines, no lists to be printed out, no urgent phone calls to be returned. Slowly the tight spring inside me began to unwind.

During those months away I learned what it felt like to not be worried all the time, and I resolved that when I got home I would try my best not to start worrying again. When I returned to the monastery refreshed and relaxed at the end of that year, I wasn't sure if I would really be able to keep my resolution to stop worrying so much. Then Father Edwin, the Headmaster, told me, "This was one of the best years the school's ever had." That really settled it for me; if St. Benedict's Prep could have such a great year when I wasn't even around, then obviously things didn't really depend on me that much and it made no sense for me to be so anxious about my work.

And so I did indeed stop worrying so much, and no longer approached every situation or task as a crisis, whether in the monastery, the school, or anywhere else.

You can imagine my bafflement, then, when I found out not long ago that Saint Paul made worrying an important prerequisite for entering the kingdom. The discovery began when I was reading the familiar story of Martha and Mary.

When I came to Jesus' remark, "Martha, Martha, you worry and fret over many things" (Luke 10:41), I didn't recognize either of the two Greek verbs. But since I knew the story I figured that the first one must mean, "to worry," and I decided that as a recovering worrier I might find this word worth looking up and getting to know better. So I reached for my Greek lexicon.

The first thing I found was that the Greek word *merimnaō*, "to worry" was based on the verb *merizō*, meaning "to divide, to distribute."[5] Behind the New Testament idea of "worrying," then, was the notion of "being divided"[6]—worrying divides our attention by steering us away from other perhaps more important concerns of life. This is what happened to Martha, the harried hostess in the gospel story: She had become distracted by so many worries that Jesus, her guest, had tried to calm her down. Since his itinerant ministry depended on the hospitality of people like Martha and Mary who took him into their homes, he was not criticizing her for making the necessary arrangements but for her attitude. The Greek says: "Martha, Martha, you are worrying and putting yourself in an uproar over many things, but only one is necessary" (Luke 10:41). Her attention

---

5. The verb *merimnaō* (mer-im-nah´-o), "to worry, be concerned," and the noun *merimna* (mer´-im-nah), "a worry, a care" are both based on *merizō* (mer-id´-zo), "to divide, distribute, deal out portions."

6. Paul connects "to worry" with "to divide" when he is making his case for virginity: "An unmarried man is anxious about [*merimnaō*] the things of the Lord, how he may please the Lord. But a married man is anxious about [*merimnaō*] the things of the world, how he may please his wife, and he is divided [*merizō*]" (1 Corinthians 7:32–34).

was so divided by performing the many duties of hospitality that she completely forgot to accept the gift he was trying to give her: his divine presence.

I smiled ruefully when I remembered how my worrying used to divide me like that, too. I would be so busy fretting about balancing class sizes and solving schedule puzzles that I wouldn't notice Jesus' presence in the student who came to me to have his schedule fixed. If he needed a kind smile or a word of encouragement, he seldom got it from me—I was too preoccupied and anxious over "important things."

But there was more to this New Testament idea of worrying. Out of curiosity I looked up the other passages where *merimnaō*, "to worry, to be anxious" is used. That was when I discovered Paul's approach to anxiety: He taught that there is a kind of anxiousness that actually makes us better Christians. He tells the Christians of Philippi, for example, that he hopes to send them Timothy, the only one who is concerned about [*merimnaō*] them the way Paul himself is (Philippians 2:20). Then, in a list of his sufferings as an apostle, Paul proudly includes along with shipwrecks, floods, hunger, and thirst, his "anxiety [*merimna*] for all the churches" (2 Corinthians 11:28). And in a powerful passage he uses the word to indicate how we, as members of Christ's body, should behave toward one another: "But God has so arranged the body, giving the greater honor to the inferior member, that there may be no dissension within the body, but the members may have the same care [*merimnaō*] for one another" (1 Corinthians 12:24–25).

In Paul's eyes, to be deeply concerned and even anxious about our brothers and sisters is, in fact, the way we ought to feel toward one another as Christians—it's the only way for us to get into the kingdom!

So, when I'm having an occasional "Martha" moment, Jesus often finds a way to remind me, "Albert, Albert, you are worried and in an uproar about many things, but only one is necessary—to love me in the people around you." And Paul adds, "You need to be concerned and anxious for all of them, especially the ones who are difficult or who demand a lot of your time and energy."

The lack of new members coming to join our monastic community will continue to be a concern. So as my brothers and I continue living our community life by loving one another as best we can, we also keep looking for opportunities to attract new members. I suppose that there are steps that we're missing at the moment, but worrying is not one of them.

Reflection

1. Think of one present worry of yours and reflect on how it "divides" your attention. What are the things it distracts you from?

2. In 1 Cor 12:25, Paul teaches that the members of Christ's body should "worry about" each other. Who are the people you worry most about? How much of this worry is healthy concern, and how much is needless, distracting anxiety? Is there perhaps someone you worry about too much? On the other hand, is there another person for whom the Lord may want you to feel more concern than you do?

Sacred Scripture

In Matt 6:25–34 some form of *merimnaō*, "to worry" occurs half a dozen times, including "Let tomorrow worry about itself."

The word "worry" appears as either a noun or a verb in Ps. 55:23; Matt 10:19; Mark 4:18–19; Luke 8:14, 12:26, 21:34; 2 Cor 11:28; and Phil 2:20, 4:6 ("Have no anxiety at all [= do not worry]").

Rule of Benedict

Great care and concern are to be shown in receiving the poor people and pilgrims, because in them more particularly Christ is received (Chapter 53, "The Reception of Guests," v. 15).

19. Getting Passionate

THE MONK WHO WAS LEADER OF PRAYER for the week was bringing Morning Prayer to a close with the litany of intercessions:

"That God will bless Newark Abbey with new members we pray to the Lord."

"Lord, hear our prayer."

Twice a day, at morning and evening prayer, we monks had included a petition like this in our common prayer. We'd been doing so for a few years now, but so far neither our prayers nor our recruiting efforts had shown any positive results.

Most believers, I thought to myself, have at one time or another experienced the frustration of having their prayers go unanswered, or gotten impatient when God seemed in no particular hurry to answer their prayers. But what should we do then? Should we just stop praying and wait politely for an answer from the Lord? Jesus once offered his disciples some advice "on the necessity for them to pray always without becoming weary" (Luke 18:1). He told them a parable about a corrupt judge and a certain widow.

The judge was part of a judicial system rife with bribery and corruption and that favored the rich and the powerful over the weak and the poor. The widow, on the other hand, was in a particularly vulnerable situation; when she lost her husband she had also lost her status in society. There was no welfare system or Social Security for her to fall back on, so she had to fend for herself as best she could, which is exactly what she was doing when she appeared before the unsuspecting judge.

On the surface the story of her clash with the judge seems straightforward enough, but in fact there are some lively and even humorous images beneath the surface of the original Greek.

The parable begins with the widow coming to the judge to demand justice against her opponent. In the original language the verb "came" is in the imperfect tense, which is Greek's way of expressing a repeated action: "she kept coming and coming." We get the idea that the woman intends to just keep badgering the judge until she gets what she wants.

Then suddenly the story comes to a speedy conclusion in a single sentence: "For a while [the judge] refused; but later he said to himself, 'Though I have no fear of God and no respect for anyone, yet because this widow keeps bothering me, I will grant her justice, so that she may not wear me out by continually coming'" (Luke 18:4–5). In the original this sentence is both more picturesque and perhaps more instructive. First, there is the expression "this widow keeps causing me trouble." The word *kopos*, "trouble"[7] comes from the root *kop-*, "to chop, hack." And this expression too is in the imperfect tense, implying constant repetition. Imagine! This powerful judge felt that he was getting chopped and hacked by this supposedly helpless woman!

"For an end to all racial and religious discrimination in our country, we pray to the Lord." Our morning's petitions kept pouring out in relentless succession.

"Lord, hear our prayer," we answered with one enthusiastic voice.

The parable ends with another forceful image: the judge decides "I will grant her justice, so that she may not wear me out" (Luke 18:5). The verb translated here as "to wear someone out" is *hupōpiazō*, literally "to strike below the eye"[8]; it is used in describing fistfights.[9] It seems the judge is afraid that the determined widow may haul off and literally sock him in the eye!

---

7. *Kopos* (kop´-os), "difficulty, toil, trouble."

8. *Hupōpiazō* (hoop-o-pee-ad´-zo), "to strike;" from *hupo*, "under" and *ops*, "the eye."

9. Paul uses this word to describe his own spiritual self-discipline: "I do not fight as if I were shadowboxing. No, I drive my body and train [*hupōpiazō*] it" (1 Corinthians 9:27). He toughens his body the way a prizefighter does, by striking it repeatedly to get it in shape.

This three-sentence parable paints an unforgettable picture of a completely powerless person managing to get her way with a mighty judge. Then Jesus draws the lesson for his hearers, including all of us: "Listen to what the unjust judge says. And will not God grant justice to his chosen ones who cry to him day and night? Will he delay long in helping them? I tell you, he will quickly grant justice to them" (Luke 18:6–8).

The phrase "who cry out to him" is a present participle in Greek, literally "calling out to him" day and night. Once again we have the image of constant relentless asking—but this time the constant calling out in prayer is to be done by you and me.

"That the Lord may move the hearts of leaders of nations to work toward a just and lasting peace in the world, we pray to the Lord." Now that's another petition that we've been repeating for decades with little noticeable effect, I grumble. But the example of the widow is a powerful reminder to me not to give up easily.

In fact, sometimes when I'm praying for something and am about to cut short my period of prayer, I hear the widow's voice whispering, "What? Are you finished already? Don't stop now, you're just getting started!" I begin to squirm as she continues, "Listen, you just go back and ask again!" She sounds so upset that I'm afraid she's going to haul off and hit me. "Then after that," she goes on, "go back and ask again. Keep asking!" Usually it seems wise to go back and do what she says.

The other day she interrupted me right in the middle of a prayer. "Listen! Do you really *want* those new vocations you're praying for? Because if you do, you sure don't sound like it! You're just rattling on, only half thinking about what you're saying. You ask that way and expect God to answer you? You've got to be kidding!" She didn't stop, but just kept coming and coming: "You've got to throw your whole heart into it! Don't be shy—that never gets results. Maybe try getting a little loud. You know—make a scene like I did with that crooked judge; let God know you're serious. Keep after him every day, every hour, every minute. And, above all, don't give up!"

St. Benedict seems to recommend the widow's approach to prayer in his *Rule*. At the beginning of the Prologue, he writes, "Every time you begin a good work, you must pray to him most earnestly to bring it to perfection" (Rule of Benedict, Prologue 4). The Latin says "*instantissime oratione*," "with most insistent prayer." In other places Benedict connects prayer with tears and compunction,[10] and advises us to pray without ceasing and throw ourselves passionately into our prayer. He says "if at other times someone chooses to pray privately, he may simply go [into the oratory] and pray, not in a loud voice, but with tears and heartfelt devotion" (RB 52:4).

And so as we keep trying to think of other ways of attracting new monks, we also keep praying that the Lord will bless our efforts. And until that starts to happen, the Almighty is going to have to listen twice a day to our persistent prayer for vocations. Maybe we'll eventually start to sound like that pesky widow who got what she wanted because the judge got tired of listening to her.

It certainly seems worth a try.

Reflection

1. Do you ever pray passionately and repeatedly for a particular intention? If so, what do you pray for? If not, what keeps you from praying that way? What do you do if your prayers are not answered? How quickly do you give up trying?

2. Most of us have been taught to pray to God tentatively, that is, to add at the end of our petitions some statement like, "However, Lord, if you don't want to grant my request, that's fine too. I will gladly accept whatever it is that you decide to do." How does this accepting, seemingly disinterested attitude during prayer square with the widow's forceful approach that was recommended by Jesus himself?

---

10. In the Rule of Benedict, prayer is twice mentioned in the same sentence with "tears."

Sacred Scripture

The Psalms contain many examples of insistent, forceful prayer. Psalm 86, for example, begins, "Incline your ear, O Lord, and answer me, for I am poor and needy. Preserve my life, for I am devoted to you; save your servant who trusts in you. You are my God; be gracious to me, O Lord, for to you do I cry all day long" (Ps 86: 1–3). Compare this with Luke 11:5–10: "Ask and it will be given to you, etc."

Rule of Benedict

Every time you begin a good work, you must pray to him with most insistent prayer to bring it to perfection (Prologue, v. 4).

20. Opening Up

I WAS COVERING A CLASS OF SENIORS; their teacher had been called out for a family emergency and told me to give the students a study hall. Seniors are always great, they actually take advantage of the extra time to study. Sitting at the teacher's desk in the front of the room, I picked up a copy of the school newspaper. A front-page headline asked in bold type, "Has God Stopped Calling People?" The subtitle was "Lack of Vocations in the Monastery Raises Concerns." As I read it I saw that it was an intelligent and sensitive article. The student reporter had interviewed a few monks, and especially the Director of Vocations. So, I thought, the monks of Newark Abbey are not the only ones wondering what's going to happen if the number of monks keeps declining.

I thought of the title of an article I once read in a Catholic magazine that also asked a question about the decline in vocations: "What Vocations Crisis?" The gist of the article had been that if a community that once had 300 members now had only 75, one need not conclude that the members were doing something wrong or that God was abandoning them. The author argued that it may be that the Lord was now expecting that group to seek and serve God as a community of 75 rather than a community of 300. But letting go of the ideal of the "good old days" when everything was "the way it was supposed to be" is not easy. And even if one is willing to let go of the past, adjusting to the new circumstances requires a kind of creativity and vision that are foreign to many religious and their superiors.

I kept reading the newspaper article while keeping an eye on my charges, who seemed to be intent on their work.

I asked myself, if Newark Abbey has fourteen members who are praying and working together peacefully, who care about one another and help one other and lots of other people to get to heaven, maybe God doesn't see this as a crisis. Maybe this is exactly what the Lord has in mind for us right now. Maybe we are being invited to envision new, unheard of possibilities that could only be seen from this new position in which we find ourselves. Maybe it's more of an invitation than a "crisis."

The real "crisis" would be if we let ourselves get discouraged, and so were no longer able to see and accept new possibilities. A real "crisis" would be if we kept looking back longingly, wishing we could return to the good old days when there were more of us. A real "crisis" would be if we were each to close inward on ourselves and stop caring lovingly for others or stop being open to God.

I stood up to stretch my bad back, and then walked around the room for a few moments on an inspection tour.

As I sat down again I thought how necessary it is for us to stay open to new possibilities and opportunities. I thought of a Greek word which I'd meditated on so many times that it was like an old friend—a helpful friend, too. The New Testament word *dianoigō*, "to open"[11] is used in such a wide variety of passages that it gives a pretty good summary of what a Christian is called to be and do.

Take, for example, how it runs throughout the story of Christ's appearance to the two disciples on the road to Emmaus (Luke 24:13–35), in which it is used three separate times. You recall that on the first Easter day, two discouraged disciples were making their way home to the village of Emmaus when suddenly Christ appeared and walked along with them, conversing with them and explaining the Scriptures. When evening started to fall, the two disciples invited the stranger to come in and stay with them. As the three were seated at supper

11. *Dianoigō* (dee-an-oy´-go), "to open, to open wide," comes from *dia-* (an intensifier) and *anoigō*, "to open."

together, Jesus blessed the bread, broke it, and gave it to them. "With
that their eyes were opened [*dianoigō*] and they recognized him" (Luke
24:31). While walking with them on the road, the risen Jesus had been
a stranger to them because he didn't fit their preconceptions—they had
not been looking for a failed Messiah, and they were certainly not open
to the possibility of a suffering and crucified Savior.

Then, as soon as their eyes were opened and they recognized Jesus,
he vanished from their sight; at this point they said to one another,
"Were not our hearts burning within us while he spoke to us on the
way and opened [*dianoigō*] the scriptures to us?" (v. 32).[12] This time it
was not their eyes that had been opened, but God's inspired word.

Then they ran all the way back to Jerusalem to the room where
the apostles were assembled, and started telling their story. While
they were still speaking, Jesus appeared in their midst, greeted them
and told them not to be afraid, and "then he opened [*dianoigō*] their
minds to understand the scriptures. And he said to them, 'Thus it is
written that the Messiah would suffer and rise from the dead on the
third day . . .'" (v. 45). Once again, "opening" was connected with the
mystery of Christ's redemptive suffering and death. This time it was the
disciples' minds that were opened to the saving truth.

The classroom was getting stuffy, so I stood up and walked over
and opened the window next to the teacher's desk. A cool, refreshing
breeze rushed in. I stood there breathing in the fresh air.

Luke continued the theme of "opening" in the Acts of the
Apostles. For instance, as Lydia listened to Paul in Philippi, "the Lord
opened [*dianoigō*] her heart to pay attention to what Paul was saying"
(Acts 16:14). This time it was someone's heart that was opened, so that
she could hear Paul's message about Christ. In the next verse she and
her whole household were baptized.

---

12. The word is used in this way also in Acts 17:3 to describe Paul's preaching in
Thessalonika, "expounding and explaining (literally *dianoigō*, "opening) the scriptures," namely, that "the Messiah had to suffer and rise from the dead."

I stood at the open window enjoying the chilly breeze and the view of downtown Newark and thinking that it was pretty obvious that, just as when St. Benedict's Prep closed in 1972, the Lord was asking us monks once again to open our hearts to a new situation. We certainly hadn't planned for either situation to happen, nor did we find either one particularly enjoyable. But the so-called "vocations crisis" was another opportunity for us to have our minds opened to the new possibilities arising from our new position, and, while doing so, to have our hearts opened in love so that we can serve one another, our students, our parishioners, and everyone who relies on us to bear witness to the Good News.

I heard behind me the sound of books closing and conversations starting. I turned away from the window and glanced at the clock: The period had flown by.

"Thank you, gentlemen," I said as the students stood and started walking toward the door.

I turned to close the window. But the fresh air was such a treat that I changed my mind. Instead, I put both hands under the half-opened window and heaved it upward all the way. I walked out leaving it wide open.

Reflection

1. Think of a time when God opened your eyes, your heart, or your mind. Was this a comfortable experience? Disconcerting? Joyous?
2. Do you tend by nature to be more open or more closed to new experiences, to meeting new people and so on? In what circumstances would you say that you are most open to God?

Sacred Scripture

Verbs for "to open" [*dianoigō* or *anoigō*] appear in the Acts of the Apostles in a few other passages that offer additional food for meditation: Acts 5:19; Acts 7:54; and Acts 14:27.

Anoigō is used in Ezekiel's promise, "I am going to open [*anoigō*] your graves" (Ezek 37:12), and Matthew shows us that prophecy fulfilled as Jesus dies on the cross: "The earth quaked, rocks were split, tombs were opened and the bodies of many who had fallen asleep were raised" (Matt 27:51–52).

Rule of Benedict

Let us open our eyes to the light that comes from God, and our ears to the voice from heaven that every day calls out (Prologue, v. 9).

CHAPTER SIX

THE KEY TO TROUBLED TIMES

The Paschal Mystery

T he major assumption that underlies this book is that if we wish to survive and indeed profit from walking our "valleys of darkness," then we need to keep in mind that our sufferings are our special way of sharing in Christ's passion, death, and resurrection, the "paschal mystery." This final chapter, then, instead of describing some specific period of struggle, looks at four occasions when I became aware of the paschal mystery at work in my life. A saintly old monk showed me what it means to witness to the risen Lord, a group of little children gave me a glimpse of Easter joy, the congregation in an African-American church shared with me a vision of Christ's victory in the midst of a tragic disaster, and a young monk professing his vows reminded me of the paschal dimension of my own monastic commitment.

21. Witnessing to the Risen Lord: Father Maurus

I KNOCKED ON THE DOOR of the monastery's sickroom, not expecting to hear an answer. I opened the door slowly and peeked in to see the old monk sitting up in bed, propped up by some pillows.

"Hi, Father Maurus!" I called cheerfully. "I hope you're feeling okay today."

Father Maurus McBarron, O.S.B., had lived a varied and active life. For many years he had served as a chaplain in the U.S. Army, he had taught in our school, and at an age when most men would have retired he had become pastor of St. Mary's, the inner city parish attached to the abbey church. In that role he became loved and respected throughout the city during the painful years of civil unrest and urban decay. But what made the biggest impression on me was the way he was living the final days of his life, debilitated by ALS, "Lou Gehrig's Disease."

I walked over to the bed and took his hand in mine for a minute, trying not to think too much about what it must be like to be slowly suffocating to death. "How's it going?" I asked.

Since his lungs were not giving him much breath to speak with, he just stared straight ahead and gave a funny little "Bronx cheer" with his pursed lips, his eloquent way of saying that he was frustrated.

"Yeah, I hear you, Father!" was all I could think of in response.

This time he gave a shrug and a weak smile. Then he turned his head and looked down expectantly at the book I was holding in my other hand.

"Oh," I said, letting go of his hand, "I brought this book for us to look at for awhile if you want. It's a history of the city of Newark. It's got some great old pictures. Want to see some of them?" For the past year or so, he and I had enjoyed reminiscing about his childhood or his days as a chaplain during World War II, or any other memories that came to mind.

He nodded, forming the word "Sure!" with his lips. So I pulled a chair alongside his bed, near the head, and sat down. I flipped open to a picture of Broad Street Newark in the 1920s and laid the book on his lap, tilting it so he could see it. "Do you remember when Broad Street looked like this?" I asked.

His eyes sparkled in recognition as he studied the old photo, and I could almost see all the memories of childhood shopping trips and streetcar rides materializing from the long-ago past. Three months earlier we would have had a lively discussion about his recollections, but now, with the disease relentlessly cutting off his breath, I had to supply the commentary. I pointed to different buildings and asked questions so that he could signal "yes" or "no" with a movement of his head. I could see how hard it was for him to be bursting with wonderful stories to tell, but not having the breath to communicate them. We did this for ten minutes or so and then suddenly his eyelids got heavy and his head drooped onto his chest. I could take a hint.

I gently took the open book and laid it on my lap and just sat there quietly with him. After a few minutes I flipped to the next page and saw a picture of the stately Essex County Courthouse that stands one block up the street from the monastery. My mind wandered back to the day when, as a student at St. Benedict's Prep, I had walked over to watch my father, a lawyer, in action during a trial. At supper that night we had talked about strategies for questioning a witness.

As happens to me more frequently than I normally admit, when I looked at Father Maurus a Greek word actually popped into my head: the word for "witness," *martus*.[1] It is used in the gospels in phrases such as "every fact may be established on the testimony of two or three witnesses [*marturoi*]" (Matthew 18:6) or "The high priest tore his robes and said, 'What further need have we of witnesses [*marturoi*]?'" (Matthew 26:65).

---

1. *Martus* (mar´-toos; plural *marturoi*) means "witness"; the verb form is *marturomai* (mar-too´-rom-ahee), "testify, be a witness." The noun *marturia* (mar-tooree´-ah) means "testimony."

So many of the first Christians paid with their lives for witnessing to Christ and his resurrection that the word for "witness" was linked with bloodshed even in the earliest days of the church—and the Greek *martus* gave us our English word "martyr." In the New Testament it's often hard to tell which way to translate the word. Paul, for instance, had told Christ during a vision, "and when the blood of your witness [*martus*] Stephen was being shed, I myself stood by giving my approval . . ." (Acts 22:20).

Christ's first followers were constantly aware that they were *marturoi,* witnesses to his resurrection. In the first Christian communities the word "witness" was practically a synonym for anyone who followed Jesus' teachings. When the apostles were choosing someone to replace Judas, for instance, Peter said that they had to find someone "to become with us a witness [*martus*] to his resurrection" (Acts 1:22).[2]

Speaking of witnesses, I thought to myself, Maurus has spent his life witnessing to the resurrection. As an Army chaplain in France shortly after the Normandy landings, he had witnessed to the hope of eternal life and God's loving forgiveness when he said mass and heard the confessions of lonely, frightened GIs. As pastor of our inner city parish he had joined with a group of local ministers to walk into the nearby housing projects during the 1967 riots, acting as a courageous witness of God's gentle love to people who were seething with pent-up anger and frustration.

I glanced at his sleeping form. Definitely a good witness. His chest was barely moving with his breathing. It occurred to me that by patiently putting up with the frustration and the terrifying shortness of breath that would eventually kill him, he was surely giving his greatest witness yet to the resurrection, to the fact that Jesus had conquered sin and death and was present right here in this room. This must certainly

---

2. Acts uses *martus* at least ten more times to refer to members of the early church, without reference to anyone's being killed for the faith (see the list in the Sacred Scripture section at the end of this chapter).

qualify him as a witness, maybe even a "martyr." He stirred a little in his bed, but then went right back to sleep.

I started to realize, as if for the first time, that our first task as Christians is to be *marturoi*, witnesses to the resurrection, just as the first Christians were. What kind of witness am I, I wondered, when I'm frustrated with my students in the classroom? When I'm feeling overwhelmed, or when I'm frightened, as Father Maurus must certainly be, do I witness to Christ's Easter peace and joy the way this old monk does?

I quietly closed the book and stood up. As I thought about his terrible difficulty breathing, I automatically took a deep breath, filling my lungs—as if the extra air might help my old friend. I gave his hand a quick squeeze and turned toward the door with a quiet prayer that someday I would be as good a witness as he was.

Reflection

1. Who are the people for whom the Risen Lord probably expects you to bear witness most often? Is that easier to do with some people than with others?

2. Have you ever taken a risk and been a witness to some unpopular value or belief? What did it cost you? When is it most difficult for you to bear witness to what you believe?

Sacred Scripture

1. In the following passages the word *martus* can be translated as either witness or martyr: "You did not deny your faith in me even in the days of Antipas my witness [*martus*], my faithful one, who was killed among you" (Rev 2:13); "And I saw that the woman was drunk with the blood of the saints and the blood of the witnesses [*marturoi*] to Jesus" (Rev 17:6).

2. In the Acts of the Apostles, Luke often uses *martus* in the sense of "witness" simply as a synonym for a follower of Jesus: Acts 1:21–22, 2:32, 3:15, 5:32, 7:58, 10:39, 10:41, 13:31, 22:15, 22:22, and 26:16.

Wisdom of the Desert

Abba Poeman said, "There is no greater love than that a man lays down his life for his neighbor. When you hear someone complaining and you struggle with yourself and do not answer him back with complaints; when you are hurt and bear it patiently, not looking for revenge; then you are laying down your life for your neighbor."[3]

---

3. Benedicta Ward, ed., *The Desert of the Heart* (London: Darton, Longman and Todd, 1988), 28.

22. Surprised by Joy

"**THE BODY OF CHRIST** . . . *El cuerpo de Cristo.*"

I was distributing Holy Communion to the members of the small Sunday congregation during the bilingual mass in Saint Augustine's Church, Newark, with the deacon standing at my left doing the same.

There was a second ritual, too, happening along with the distribution of the Eucharist: the blessing of children who weren't old enough to receive Holy Communion. In fact, most of those on my line were little ones—and a few adults too—coming to receive a blessing.

That morning for some reason I was especially aware of God's beauty shining in the children's upturned faces, their simple smiles and laughing eyes. I felt overwhelming delight and love welling up in my heart as God's beautiful children kept coming forward to receive their blessing and a gentle touch on the head.

Next in line was one of the littlest ones; she seemed to know instinctively how to melt someone's heart with her smile. I bent way down and peered into her wide eyes, struggling to keep from laughing with sheer enjoyment. I made the sign of the cross over her head: "May the Lord bless you and keep you always, in the name of the Father and of the Son and of the Holy Spirit. Amen." Then I placed my hand gently on her head of jet-black hair as her "big" brother stood behind her, a protective hand on each of her shoulders.

I looked forward each Sunday to this delightful if unofficial sacrament for children. But there was more happening there than you could see, because each child who came up for my blessing was unknowingly blessing *me* in return.

That particular morning I could feel each of them blessing me with God's gift of joy. "I know what this is," I said to myself, "this is *chara*." One of my best "friends" from the New Testament, *chara*[4] means "delight, joy,

---

4. *Chara* (khar-ah´).

gift, grace, being favored by God." And that morning I was experiencing every one of these, all at once. Yes, this was definitely *chara*!

The children kept coming up in single file, and I kept making the sign of the cross over each, and they kept blessing me with their laughing eyes and captivating smiles. None of them had ever heard the word *chara*, of course, but they were surely offering it to me in all its senses: God's favor and grace, a freely given gift, and most of all joy.

The words "joy," "rejoice," and "favor"[5] keep echoing like a beautiful refrain throughout the New Testament. Words based on the root verb "*char-*" appear several times in the infancy narratives of Luke and Matthew,[6] and joy continues as a major theme throughout Jesus' public life. Jesus once told a parable about joy, "The kingdom of heaven is like a treasure buried in a field, which a person finds and hides again, and out of joy [*chara*] goes and sells all that he has and buys that field" (Matt 13:44). The noun *chara* normally means "a sense of calm delight," but sometimes, as in that story, it can make you forget yourself, throw your hands in the air and do extravagant things, such as let go of everything else and accept the kingdom with all your heart. That was the kind of delight I was feeling that morning as I was being blessed by dozens of children. I was ready to throw my hands in the air and shout.

Oops! I had started to bless an eight-year-old girl when her insulted expression reminded me that I should be giving her communion instead of treating her like a child. We both smiled at our secret joke as I offered her the host: "The body of Christ."

The next person in line was an older woman who had spoken to me just last week. Her heart was broken because her son back in South

---

5. Verb forms are *chairō* (khah´-ee-ro), "rejoice, be glad" and *charitoō*, (khar-ee-to´-o), "to favor someone," and nouns are *chara* (khar-ah´), "joy, delight" and *charis* (khar-ees´), "grace; favor."

6. See the Sacred Scripture at the end of this chapter for a complete list.

America had recently told her on the phone to stop calling. He had informed her angrily that he wanted nothing more to do with her, and that he would no longer answer any of her calls. I remembered looking into her tearful face and wishing that my Spanish were a little better so I could offer her more eloquent words of comfort than the simple ones I had managed to come up with.

Yet now when that unfortunate woman approached to receive communion she was smiling, and I could sense the joy and consolation that she felt as she received her Lord in the Eucharist. We traded glances of recognition as I said "*El cuerpo de Cristo*" and offered her the host.

Her experience of joy in the midst of sorrow made her, I thought, like the apostles at the Last Supper. In John's account of that final meal, an event filled with sadness and foreboding, Jesus kept speaking to the disciples about joy, assuring them that their sorrow would one day be transformed. "When a woman is in labor, she has pain, because her hour has come. But when her child is born, she no longer remembers the anguish because of the joy [*chara*] of having brought a human being into the world. So you have pain now; but I will see you again, and your hearts will rejoice [*chairō*], and no one will take your joy [*chara*] from you" (John 16:21–22). The contrast between the woman's present labor pains and her future joy was Jesus' way of teaching us how joy can come out of pain and anxiety.

My parishioner friend knew what labor pains were. As she turned after receiving communion I hoped that she would be able find strength in Jesus' promise that out of pain can eventually come joy.

But joy is not just something awaiting us in heaven. Jesus made it clear that he wanted all of us to have this gift right now: "I have said these things to you so that my joy [*chara*] may be in you, and that your joy [*chara*] may be complete" (John 15:11). In fact, joy is one of the fruits of the Holy Spirit: "The fruit of the Spirit is love, joy [*chara*], peace, patience, kindness, generosity. . . ." (Galatians 5:22). We shouldn't be surprised, then, when we experience the joy of the Lord in the love of people around us, in the beauties of nature, or in the closeness to God that we may feel during prayer or when receiving a sacrament. But sometimes joy surprises us at a time when we most need it and are least expecting it—even as we're walking through some dark valley.

By now the woman was almost back at her seat, and the last of the little ones was standing in front of me craning her neck upward waiting expectantly. I raised my hand and began to say the blessing, trying to stay in my solemn, priestly role; but as I looked at her beautiful innocent face and into her sparkling eyes, any pretense of priestly gravity broke down and—I couldn't help myself—I laughed. Out of sheer *chara*.

Reflection

1. Are there experiences that have filled you with "the joy of the Lord?" If so, reflect on one of them and thank the Lord for it.
2. The New Testament mentions people experiencing joy in the face of suffering (Acts 5:41; Col 1:24). Reflect on this seeming contradiction. Has that ever happened to you?

Sacred Scripture

Words based on the root verb *chairō*, "to be joyful" appear seven times in the infancy narratives of Luke. The angel Gabriel announces to Zechariah: "And you will have joy [*chara*] and gladness, and will rejoice [*chairō*] at his birth" (Luke 1:14) and greets Mary: "Hail ([*chairō*]—literally "Rejoice") highly favored one [*charitoō*]" (Luke 1:28). Then the angel announces to the shepherds (in a literal translation), "Behold, I proclaim to you a great joy [*chara*] that will be for all the people" (Luke 2:10). Matthew tells us that when the star they had been following came to a stop over the place where the child was, the magi literally "rejoiced [*chairō*] with joy [*chara*]" (Matt 2:10).

Rule of Benedict

During these days [of Lent], therefore, we will add to the usual measure of our service something by way of private prayer and abstinence from food or drink, so that each of us will have something above the assigned measure to offer God of his own will with the joy of the Holy Spirit (Chapter 49, "The Observance of Lent," vv. 5–6).

23. Lifted Up with Christ

I WAS FILLING IN THAT SUNDAY MORNING for the vacationing pastor of Queen of Angels Church, an African-American parish not far from the monastery. The ten o'clock mass was filled as usual with spirit and energy thanks to the exuberant singing of the gospel choir and the rich, lively chords that the organist was coaxing from the old pipe organ.

I had just finished proclaiming the gospel, and now I walked to the center of the sanctuary and knelt on the floor, facing the altar, with my back to the people. The congregation and choir, still standing, began singing their customary "prayer over the preacher," asking the Holy Spirit to help me to give a powerful sermon. Kneeling there I realized that I really needed their prayers in a special way that day, Sunday, September 16, 2001. Just a few days before, about fourteen miles from that spot, the two World Trade towers had collapsed and disappeared in clouds of smoke like a vision of hell itself. The horrendous images of the collapsing infernos were still being replayed constantly on television—and in everyone's mind. Millions of people around the country and around the world were still stunned by the enormity and horror of the tragedy.

As I knelt there the chorus of the traditional hymn filled the church: "Sweet Holy Spirit, sweet heav'nly dove, stay right here with us, filling us with your love. . . ." I sensed that the people at mass that morning were hoping for a word or two of encouragement to help them deal with last Tuesday's immense, unthinkable catastrophe. I realized that this was not going to be an easy time to preach, so I was grateful for their prayers, and added a few of my own. When the hymn ended I stood up and walked slowly back to the pulpit, hoping that I might find a word of hope to offer the church. As it turned out, I did indeed find a word—quite literally.

I began by reminding everyone that two days ago the church had celebrated the solemn feast of the Exaltation of the Holy Cross. In my own meditation on the readings for that feast, I told the listening congregation, I had drawn a lot of comfort from the passage "And when I am lifted up from the earth, I will draw everyone to myself" (John 12:32–34). In fact, since then I had been meditating on one particular word in that sentence. And so I started to share as best I could some thoughts about the verb *hupsoō*,[7] "to lift up." Let me tell you a little about this extraordinarily interesting word.

Most of the time in the New Testament it was used figuratively for "lifting" someone to a position of honor or power: "Whoever exalts [*hupsoō*] himself will be humbled, and whoever humbles himself will be exalted [*hupsoō*]" (Matthew 23:12). But John used it in its literal sense when referring to a scene from the book of Numbers: "Moses lifted up [*hupsoō*] the serpent in the desert" (John. 3:14a).[8] This literal use of "to lift up" in the Old Testament provided John with exactly the image he needed to express Christ's being physically "lifted up" on the cross: he wrote "And just as Moses lifted up [*hupsoō*] the serpent in the desert, so must the Son of Man be lifted up [*hupsoō*] so that everyone who believes in him may have eternal life" (John 3:14–15).

One of the doors at the rear of the church opened quietly and three people came in and slipped into a back pew.

With his love for double meanings, John would continue this image of "lifting up" later on, in Jesus' ambiguous promise, "And when I am lifted up [*hupsoō*] from the earth, I will draw everyone to myself" (John 12:32–34). Did this "being lifted up" refer to Christ's being literally lifted up onto the cross, or to his finally being lifted up in glory to the right hand of God in heaven? Or did it refer to both at the same time? John's

---

7. *Hupsoō* (hoop-so´-oh), "to lift up, exalt, elevate to a place of honor," from *huper*, "above."

8. This a reference to the story in Numbers 21:4–9 in which Moses fashions a bronze serpent so that the Israelites who are being punished by being bitten by "fiery serpents" can gaze on the bronze figure and be healed.

deliberate ambiguity pointed up the mysterious nature of the crucifixion and of all human suffering. But he also gave us a central insight about human suffering when he wrote that, by being lifted up on the cross, Christ "draws all to himself" (John 12:32–33): Calvary was just the first step in a process. After being "lifted up" onto the cross Jesus would then be "lifted up" out of death by his Father and finally raised on high to sit at the right hand of the Father. And—here is the crucial point—we too are to be lifted up along with him as he draws us all to himself.

As I scanned the faces in the pews, I was encouraged by the number of interested expressions. I could sense that they were listening and, I hoped, starting to get the point of my sermon: the link between our own suffering and Christ's triumphing over his suffering and death on the cross.

John, by playing on the double meaning of "lifted up," deftly links our human suffering with the mystery of Calvary, and then, with the cross as the starting point, describes a single upward surge in which all of creation—including our darkest valleys of sin and suffering—is embraced by Christ and lifted heavenward by him and with him in the vast, infinite, and inexorable power of divine unconditional love.

Thus, Christ's cross becomes the very means by which all of us, too, are lifted to salvation. Suffering is a mysterious but somehow integral part of the ceaseless upward movement of divine love.

I then shared with the congregation a powerful image that had come to me early that very morning as I was praying over what to say in that sermon. My vision began with the now too-familiar image of the Twin Towers collapsing amid billows of dust and smoke, but it didn't end there: When the collapsing buildings had crashed into the earth there was a momentary pause, and the whole world fell silent, as if in shock. Then slowly the towers began to be lifted back up, and then all of Manhattan started to be drawn upward after

them in a single mighty surge. Next the entire New York metropolitan area, including Newark and Queen of Angels church, was swept upward, then the whole country, until finally the whole world with all its misery and pain, all of its sin and suffering, began to be lifted heavenward as well, caught up in the relentless, irresistible power of Christ's infinite, unconditional, and universal love. He was keeping his promise: "When I am lifted up [*hupsoō*] from the earth, I will draw everyone to myself."

"Yes!" said a voice in the congregation. "All right!" agreed a member of the choir.

Heartened by their responses, I continued, telling how this vision had filled me with confidence and peace, and that I hoped that it might do the same for someone in the church that morning.

We are not able, I went on, to understand right now just how it is that the evil and suffering of our lives or the terror and the tragedy of the past week all fit into the picture, and so we pray that we may be blessed with the eyes of faith when we look upon our troubled times—just as when we look upon a crucifix. With those eyes and with the help of John's beautiful image we may be able to see that we and our dark valleys, and indeed the whole world and its struggles, are continuously being "lifted up" by Christ in that single inevitable heavenward motion, a motion that will finally be completed on that day when all creation has been transformed, and every tear wiped away, and when every evil has been overcome and every pain forgotten amid the eternal joys of heaven.

"Amen!" came a comment. "Thank you Jesus!" someone else prayed.

As I left the pulpit, my pulse still racing with the emotion of preaching, I realized just how much I had needed to hear that sermon myself. I whispered a word of thanks to the Lord as I took my seat in the celebrant's chair.

"That prayer over the preacher," I thought to myself, "is pretty powerful stuff."

Reflection

1. Think of a time of particularly intense suffering in your life. Were you eventually able to get some perspective on the situation? If so, what was it? Where did it come from?

2. The traditional Catholic practice of "offering up" the day's little inconveniences and sufferings is a way of consciously connecting your own tribulations to those of Jesus on Calvary. What small "suffering" might you offer today?

Sacred Scripture

One sentence that combines perfectly Christ's crucifixion and his exaltation in that single, upward movement of salvation is John 8:28: "Jesus said (to them), 'When you lift up [*hupsoō*] the Son of Man, then you will realize that I AM.'"[9]

Similar passages worth looking at are: Isa 52:13–15; Acts 5:30–31; and Rom 8:18–23.

Wisdom of the Desert

Abba Euprepios said, "Knowing that God is faithful and mighty, have faith in him and you will share what is his. If you are depressed, you do not believe. We all believe that he is mighty and believe that everything is possible to him. As for your own affairs, believe with faith in him about them, too, for he is able to work miracles in you also.[10]

---

9. The expression "I AM" is a reference to Ex 3:14 in which God answers Moses' question, "Who shall I say sent me?" The answer is, in one translation, "Tell them 'I AM' sent you." Jesus applies this divine name to himself in several other places in John's gospel.

10. Benedicta Ward, ed., *The Desert of the Heart* (London: Darton, Longman and Todd, 1988), 60.

24. Rising to New Life

THE LATE MORNING SUN WAS FLOODING through the stained-glass windows into the abbey church, covering the oak floor with glowing smudges of blue, red, and gold. Everyone was kneeling during the Litany of the Saints except for one young monk who was lying face down in the middle of the sanctuary. He was preparing to profess solemn monastic vows. We were all calling on the saints to help him to remain strong and faithful in his commitment to search for God with us in Newark Abbey for the rest of his life.

"Saint John the Baptist, Pray for us."

"Saint Joseph, Pray for us."

"Saint Peter and Saint Paul, Pray for us."

The ceremony had begun with an invitation from the Abbot: "My son, through baptism you have already died to sin and been consecrated to the Lord. Are you resolved to unite yourself more closely to him by the bond of solemn profession?"

Since the early days of monasticism, spiritual writers have spoken of monastic profession as a "second baptism." In baptism every Christian enters into the paschal mystery—Christ's passage through suffering and death to return to the Father—but the monk in professing his vows promises to live his baptismal promises in a more intense way, renouncing Satan and dying to himself through the practices of obedience, voluntary poverty, self-denial, and so forth.

I smiled as I remembered my own solemn vows ceremony when I had to lie prostrate in prayer. Back then there was an even clearer connection between professing vows, and dying and rising in baptism: I was actually covered, as I lay there, with a funeral pall, and six funeral candles were arranged around me while the litany was chanted.

Suddenly I was back in the present and the cantors were coming to the end of the litany:

"By your death and rising to new life, Lord, save your people."

"By your gift of the Holy Spirit, Lord, save your people."

After the litany the abbot stood up and prayed, "Lord, grant the prayers of your people. Prepare the heart of your servant for consecration to your service. By the grace of the Holy Spirit purify him from all sin and set him on fire with your love. We ask this through Christ our Lord."

As we answered "Amen" it struck me that this oration contained more baptismal language: the forgiveness of sins and the pouring out of the Spirit.

The deacon then said, "Let us rise," and everyone stood. The monk who had been lying on the floor got to his knees and then stood up. As I watched him rise to his feet I couldn't help thinking of that rich New Testament word *egeirō*.[11] Its first meaning is a simple one, describing exactly what this monk had just done: "to rise up." For example, after being warned by an angel, "Joseph got up [*egeirō*], took the child and his mother by night, and went to Egypt" (Matthew 2:14). But the young monk's gesture of rising up after the litany was, like the word *egeirō* and like the vows ceremony itself, rich with overtones of resurrection. *Egeirō's* Easter implications come across in many of Jesus' miracles.

First, *egeirō* is often connected with Jesus' healing miracles. For instance, he said to the paralytic, "'Stand up [*egeirō*], take your bed and go to your home.' And he stood up [*egeirō*] and went to his home" (Matthew 9:6–7).[12]

Second and more importantly, the word is always used when Jesus raises someone from the dead. When he saw the funeral procession of the widow's son near Naim, "he came forward and touched the bier,

---

11. *Egeirō* (*eg-i'-ro*), "to awaken, rise up, stand up."

12. Another example is, "When Jesus entered Peter's house, he saw his mother-in-law lying in bed with a fever; he touched her hand, and the fever left her, and she got up [*egeirō*] and began to serve him" (Matthew 8:14–15).

and the bearers stood still. And he said, 'Young man, I say to you, rise [*egeirō*]!'" (Luke 7:14); and when he saw the twelve-year-old daughter of Jairus lying dead "He took her by the hand and said to her, '*Talitha cum*', which means, 'Little girl, get up [*egeirō*]!' And immediately the girl got up [*egeirō*] and began to walk about" (Mark 5:41).[13] The gospel writers very deliberately choose *egeirō* to describe people "rising" from sickness and even death because they want us to see these events as foreshadowing that one greatest "arising" that will happen on Easter Sunday morning.

This brings us to the third and principal use of the verb: *egeirō* is the evangelists' preferred word for Jesus' own "rising" and "being raised" from the grave. In Matthew's version, when the women went to the tomb early on Easter morning and found it empty, an angel who was sitting there said to them, "Do not be afraid; I know that you are looking for Jesus who was crucified. He is not here; for he has been raised [*egeirō*], as he said" (Matt 28:5-6). Matthew had indeed shown Jesus predicting this very event several times: "From that time on, Jesus began to show his disciples that he must go to Jerusalem and undergo great suffering . . . and be killed, and on the third day be raised [*egeirō*]" (Matthew 16:21).[14] And John, too, tells us that "after he was raised [*egeirō*] from the dead, his disciples remembered that he had said this; and they believed the scripture and the word that Jesus had spoken" (John 2:22). The word *egeirō* is then at the very center of our Easter faith.

Now at last it was time for the monk to approach the abbot, holding the vow formula which he had written out by his own hand. He knelt down and read the formula from the sheet: "In the name of the Lord Jesus Christ, Amen. . . . I promise with solemn vows, before God and his saints, in the presence of our Father in Christ, Abbot Melvin

13. It is used in several places to refer to "Lazarus, whom he had raised [*egeirō*] from the dead" (John 12:1, see vv. 9, 17, etc.).

14. *Egeirō* is used in Matthew's other two predictions of the passion and resurrection in 17:23 and 20:19, and in Luke's version in Luke 9:22.

and the monks of this monastery, stability in this community, pursuit of perfect charity through a monastic manner of life, and obedience according to the Rule of our holy father Benedict. . . ."

Just as our community kept watch in this very place every Holy Saturday during the Easter Vigil, remembering the death of Christ and celebrating his glorious rising from the grave, so this morning this young monk was promising to be always on watch, embracing with joy the renunciations of monastic observance in order to die to himself, to live in body and soul the life of the risen Lord in the hope of one day "rising up" with Christ into the presence of the Father.

Matthew uses *egeirō* in a striking prophetic image of our own rising as he describes the moment of Jesus' death on Calvary: "The tombs also were opened, and many bodies of the saints who had fallen asleep were raised [*egeirō*] (Matthew 27:52).

The new monk was claiming by his actions that *egeirō* applied not only to Christ's resurrection, but to his own as well. He was living out what Saint Paul had written to the Romans, "Do you not know that all of us who have been baptized into Christ Jesus were baptized into his death? Therefore we have been buried with him by baptism into death, so that, just as Christ was raised [*egeirō*] from the dead by the glory of the Father, so we too might walk in newness of life" (Romans 6:3–4).

Having finished his public profession of vows, the newly professed monk now walked slowly to the altar and placing the vow formula on the book of the gospels, signed the document.

Everyone applauded as the young man finished signing his name. As I joined in the applause I prayed for him and for our monastery and for everyone in the church that morning, that we all might keep on "rising up" day after day from our failures, mistakes, and weaknesses of body and spirit. I prayed, too, that one day we might all finally arrive together in the presence of the eternal, risen, and victorious Christ to join in the new life of the eternal Easter in heaven.

Reflection

1. The gospel writers made a connection between Christ's "rising"
   at the resurrection and people's "rising" after being cured of some
   disease. Have you ever experienced some sort a "rising," a resurrection in your life? Was there another person involved in calling
   you to life?

2. Christ always uses a simple word or words to call people back to
   life. Think of someone you may have helped to "arise" from sadness or worry or pessimism by your words of encouragement.

Sacred Scripture

Egeirō, "to get up" is found in Matt 9:19 and Rom 13:11. In the sense of
"rising from the dead," it is found in many places, including John 5:21;
1 Cor 15:17; and 2 Cor 4:14.

Rule of Benedict

Let us get up then, at long last, for the scriptures rouse us when they
say: It is high time for us to arise from sleep (Prologue, v. 8).

Epilogue

I began the introduction to this book by observing, "One of the most basic of all human traits is the desire to make sense of things. We all want to know that our life has a meaning, that it has a plot." Writing this book has given me some new insights into my own story.

As I read through the nearly finished manuscript, I began to see each individual meditation in the light of all the others that came before and after it, and to discover patterns and connections that I had never noticed before. One good example is that in rereading the four reflections on the closing of Saint Benedict's Prep, I was struck by how well each meditation seemed to apply also to our monastery's current challenge of diminishing numbers. What began as a collection of twenty-four separate meditations became a single coherent story in which I can now see some more of the plot of my life. This was both a surprise and a welcome gift.

Further, writing about painful events in my life in terms of the paschal mystery has deepened my awareness and appreciation of the countless graces that the Lord has been constantly, quietly pouring out on me throughout my life.

I hope that as you have walked with me through some of the dark valleys of my life, you may have found an occasional useful insight or some little encouragement to help you deal more peacefully or fruitfully with your own troubled times. Or perhaps you may have learned from one of my helpful "friends" from the Greek New Testament some new perspective on the mysterious ways the Lord is at work in your life.

May God grant both of us the wisdom to keep discovering the mysterious divine love that surrounds us and helps us on our journey—a journey the leads up onto mountaintops and down into dark valleys—until we arrive together in the Kingdom where we will live and reign with the risen and victorious Lord for ever and ever. Amen.

Annotated Bibliography

We are blessed in our day with dozens of helpful works that can deepen our insight into the language of the New Testament. Below are just three well-known and easily available works designed to be used by the layperson with no background in Biblical Greek. Fairly inexpensive editions of each can be found in major bookstores and online.

W.E. Vine. *Vine's Complete Expository Dictionary of Old and New Testament Words. Nashville*: Thomas Nelson Publishers, 1996.

An extremely useful study aid with all sorts of indexes of biblical themes and key words in English. Individual Greek and Hebrew words are transliterated into English and followed by the spelling in the original language; newer editions also give the reference number from Strong's (see next entry) for each word, a great time saver, especially for the beginner. This work can be consulted online free of charge by typing in "Vine's online" in a search engine.

James Strong, LL.D., S.T.D. *The New Strong's Exhaustive Concordance of the Bible*. Nashville: Thomas Nelson Publishers, 1995.

For over 100 years this monumental work has been the most widely used Bible concordance ever compiled. Using the King James Version, it lists every word in context, but then offers for each a reference number referring the reader to the original word in the appropriate Greek or Hebrew dictionary at the back of the volume. This work can be consulted online free of charge by typing in "Strong's online" in a search engine.

William Barclay. *New Testament Words*. Louisville: Westminster John Knox Press, 1974.

This modest paperback studies the meaning of sixty-one New Testament words (including such important ones as *agape*, *charisma*, and *hubris*) in classical and Hellenistic Greek, the Septuagint, and other ancient sources, as well as in the New Testament. This is the book that first showed me how linguistic scholarship can be applied in our practical everyday Christian lives.

Subject Index

(Numbers refer to pages)

INDEX OF GREEK WORDS

(Numbers refer to pages)